Elementary Dynamic Programming

AF855082

Chaouki Abdallah
oct-10-1983.

Elementary Dynamic Programming

J. M. Norman

Crane, Russak & Company, Inc.
New York

© J.M. NORMAN 1975

First published 1975 by
Edward Arnold (Publishers) Ltd

Published in the United States by
Crane, Russak & Company, Inc.
347 Madison Avenue
New York, NY 10017

Library of Congress Catalog No. 75-13746
ISBN 0-8448-0719-2

All Rights Reserved. No part of this publication may be reproduced, stored in a retrieval system, or transmitted in any form or by any means, electronic, mechanical, photocopying, recording or otherwise, without the prior permission of the Publisher.

Printed in Great Britain

Preface

Dynamic programming is an optimization technique which has been developed over the past twenty years and has proved useful in a variety of practical problems. This book is intended as an introduction to the technique. The approach throughout is practical, with the emphasis on understanding the basic concepts and applying the methods. Only elementary mathematics is needed to understand this book, though Sections 2.2 and 2.3 may be found more complex.

It is hoped that the variety of examples will demonstrate the wide applicability of dynamic programming and that the book will be useful not only to the student of operational research but to the experienced manager who wants to keep in touch with developments in management science.

J.M.N.

Acknowledgements

Much of this book is derived from other sources. Many of the examples have appeared in Bellman's books and the two examples most used for exposition are adapted from the book by White, to whom is due the classification of objectives and computational methods. I hope that this book will serve as an introduction to those which they have written. The measurement puzzle in Section 3.2 is from Polya and the orchestra problem is from Mr. R.M. Adelson.

I am very grateful to Professor D.J. White, Professor M.G. Simpson and Mr. S.H. Ashcroft who kindly read the manuscript: the book is the better for their helpful comments. The faults which remain are mine.

Finally, I thank Mr. E.L. Newbigging who suggested that I write the book, Mr. L.C. Selwood of Edward Arnold for his patience while I did so, and Miss Penny Abbott who typed the manuscript.

Contents

Preface v

Acknowledgements vi

1 Fundamentals 1
- 1.1 The Principle of Optimality
- 1.2 The Concepts of Dynamic Programming

2 Formulation 10
- 2.1 Non-final Value Systems
- 2.2 Final Value Systems
- 2.3 Backward Contractions and Sensitivity Analysis

3 Other Computational Methods 48
- 3.1 Approximation in Policy Space
- 3.2 Computation for Directed States

4 Computational Problems 65
- 4.1 Dimensionality
- 4.2 Lagrange Multipliers
- 4.3 Grid Size

5 Decision Analysis 81

Further Reading 88

References 89

Index 91

1 Fundamentals

1.1 The Principle of Optimality

Overview

The uniqueness of dynamic programming lies in the principle of optimality and it is on this principle that the whole of dynamic programming is based. Just as in the calculus we use the fundamental idea of differentiating a function and equating to zero to find its minima or maxima (remembering to evaluate the function at the end points), so in dynamic programming we use the principle of optimality, expressed in the functional equation. The principle is easy enough to recite. Bellman[5] put it this way: "An optimal policy has the property that, whatever the initial state and initial decision are, the remaining decisions must constitute an optimal policy with regard to the state resulting from the first decision." As Bellman says in his first book on dynamic programming, this observation has all the dangerous simplicity of a half-truth. It is not a half-truth and it can be verified quickly enough by a proof by contradiction. It is not, however, an easy principle to grasp and it is worthwhile spending some time on a simple illustration of the idea it expresses.

Example: a routing problem

Let us consider the optimal route from Marble Arch in London to the Bull Ring in Birmingham. Before we go any further, we need to specify what we mean by the word *optimal*. This word can mean different things to different people at different times and what it denotes can depend on circumstances: what is optimal in one set of circumstances may not be optimal in another. The optimal route from Marble Arch to the Bull Ring may be the shortest route by roads on which a car can be used, but this is not the only possible meaning of the word in this context. It could be interpreted as

most direct route on foot
most scenic route less than 150 miles long
quickest route using any means of transport
fastest scheduled train route

route which would get us to the destination in ten hours stopping at the greatest number of pubs on the way

and there are many other possible interpretations.

Suppose we pick one of them: the route we would take in our own car to get us to the Bull Ring as quickly as possible. Opinions may differ but most people would agree that the optimal route, in this interpretation, would to be drive up the M1, turning on to the M6 after Crick (near Rugby) and turning on to the A38(M) at Gravelly Hill, in the Birmingham suburbs. In more detail, we might list some of the places we would go through:

Marble Arch
St. John's Wood
Hendon
Newport Pagnell
Crick
Corley
Gravelly Hill
Bull Ring

We can interpret this list in two ways: first, as a sequence of states (places where we are) and second, as a sequence of decisions following an initial state. First of all we are at Marble Arch (a state) and we make a decision (to go to St. John's Wood). When we get there we make another decision (to go to Hendon). When we get there we make another decision (to go to Newport Pagnell), and so on until we arrive at the Bull Ring. (We assume throughout that we reach each destination – our car never breaks down!)

Now let us return to the principle of optimality and interpret it in the light of this illustration.

The initial state is: Marble Arch.

The initial decision is: go to St. John's Wood.

The principle of optimality tells us that in this example, the remaining decisions:

Go to Hendon
Go to Newport Pagnell
Go to Crick
Go to Corley
Go to Gravelly Hill
Go to the Bull Ring

must constitute an optimal route from St. John's Wood to the Bull Ring, using the same interpretation of optimal. In other words, if the optimal route from Marble Arch to the Bull Ring goes through St. John's Wood, Hendon, Newport Pagnell, Crick, Corley and Gravelly Hill, then the optimal route from St. John's Wood (the state resulting from the first decision) to the Bull Ring also goes through Hendon, Newport Pagnell,

Crick, Corley and Gravelly Hill. In exactly the same way, if the optimal route from St. John's Wood to the Bull Ring goes through Hendon, Newport Pagnell, Crick, Corley and Gravelly Hill, then the optimal route from Hendon (the state resulting from the first decision in this sequence) also goes through Newport Pagnell, Crick, Corley and Gravelly Hill. And so on. One can see why White[21] could put the principle of optimality in another, neater way by stating that all contractions of an optimal policy are themselves optimal.

One can also see in this example how a proof by contradiction would work. Suppose the optimal route from St. John's Wood to the Bull Ring did not go through Hendon, Newport Pagnell and the rest, but went to the Bull Ring via some other places. Then a route from Marble Arch to St. John's Wood and through all these other places would be better than the route already given, and the route already given would consequently not be an optimal route from Marble Arch to the Bull Ring.

Conclusion

In this illustration, its application seems so obvious that one might suppose that the principle of optimality is, although true, only trivial. This is not so, but it is indeed remarkable that the recognition and application of such a simple idea can provide such a powerful tool for the solution of complex sequential decision problems.

Consider the problem of replacement of equipment – a machine, for example. Leaving aside the issue of taxation, what should concern us is the current state of the machine, what we need it for and how much it would cost us to replace it. Consequently, the amount of the purchase price of the current machine we have written off is irrelevant to the decision whether to keep or replace. Similarly, in our private lives, when we consider whether or not to sell our car, what should concern us is the future performance we can expect from the car we now own, how much we could expect to sell it for, the performance we can expect from another car we might buy and how much we would have to pay for it. The consideration of how long we have had the current car is irrelevant to the decision whether to keep or replace it. All this is not to say that past history is necessarily unimportant, simply that it is relevant only in so far as it affects the state of affairs we are in at the time we make a decision. An adequate description of the state we are in needs to take account of all the information relevant to possible future performance. It is only in this sense that the past history of a system is a part of the present state.

1.2 The Concepts of Dynamic Programming

Overview

In stating the principle of optimality, we used a number of words which we did not define, such as state, decision.and policy. In this section we shall explain what we mean by them. As in the previous section, we use an illustration.

Example: the ice-cream seller

We consider an elementary and artificial inventory problem. A student is working for a firm of ice-cream manufacturers for a month during his summer vacation, selling ice-cream from a van, and on each of his working days he follows the same routine. First thing in the morning he counts up his stock and decides how much to pick up from the manufacturer's depot in town. Having picked up this amount, he drives his van along the route that has been assigned to him, stopping in a set sequence of places, selling as much as he can of what he has available. The question he needs to answer at the beginning of each day is: how many ice-creams should he pick up from the depot? There are lots of things we have not mentioned which would be relevant to this problem and many respects in which this example is artificial. In particular, we have made no mention of costs and prices, nor have we said what the student's objectives are. Nevertheless this example will serve our purpose.

First of all, note the times at which the student considers the question at issue, namely at the beginning of each day. These decision epochs we will call *stages*. The stages in a sequential decision process are those points in time at which we consider the system and decide what, if anything, to do next. In effect, the system undergoes a sequence of transitions and the stages are a means of ordering this sequence.

The stage in this example is simply what day it is. If the student is working for the whole vacation, we could define the stage as the number of days left until the end of the vacation; if he is working for a month, we could define the stage as the number of days left until the end of the month. Notice that if we adopt this way of defining the stage, the stages run backwards in time. If the student works throughout July, then although the calendar dates will run consecutively from 1 to 31, the stages will run consecutively from 31 to 1. This convention often causes difficulty to those approaching dynamic programming for the first time. For the time being we remark that it is only a convention, but when it comes to computing the optimal policy (which is what we want to do in sequential decision problems), the convention seems eminently sensible.

In general terms, the *state* is a sufficient description of the condition of the system at a stage, relevant to its future performance; in our example, it is the number of ice-creams the student has in stock at the beginning of a day. Other things, such as the weather, the known intentions of competitors, etc. may all be important, but suppose here that the sole consideration is the number of ice-creams in stock. Thus the state of the system here is a number (i, for example).

The state of the system is not always so simply described. If the student carried several types of ice-cream, then the state of the system might be represented by (i_1, i_2, i_3, i_4) where

i_1 = number of 5p vanilla ice-creams
i_2 = number of 5p strawberry ice-creams
i_3 = number of 5p chocolate ice-creams
i_4 = number of 10p neapolitan ice-creams

The state of the system would then be a vector (i_1, i_2, i_3, i_4). A state description might even (as in the optimal route of the previous section) be the name of a place. It is impossible to lay down rules about what kind of things must enter the state description and this is part of the difficulty of model building in operational research generally; all we can say is what the state must represent, namely a sufficient description of the condition of the system relevant to future performance.

The third word we need to consider is *decision*, a topic about which whole books have been written. For our purposes, we may take a decision as being an action chosen at some stage and dependent on the state of the system. In the example the decision to be taken at the beginning of each day is to pick up from the depot a certain number of ice-creams. Symbolically, if one morning n days from the end of the month (stage) there are i ice-creams in the van (state), then the student may choose to pick up k more ice-creams from the depot (decision) and we may write

$$k = k_n(i)$$

to show that k depends on both i and n.

Fourthly, a *policy* is a decision rule, indeed some writers use policy and decision rule interchangeably. A policy is a decision rule which defines an action for every state at every stage. Thus in principle a policy can be written in the following form (Table 1.1), in which each row corresponds to a state and each column to a stage, while the entries in the table are the actions to be taken dependent on the state and the stage. More succinctly, we may say that a policy defines a k for every i at every n. A policy does not have to be optimal, indeed the example given presents some rather curious features. Nevertheless it defines an action for every state at every stage and is consequently a perfectly proper policy. With 28 days left and 6 ice-creams in the van, pick up 184; with 30 days left and 193 ice creams in the van, pick up 7; and so on. The policy embodied in the table could be expressed very simply as

on Fridays, Saturdays, Sundays, stock up to 200
on Mondays, Tuesdays, Wednesdays, Thursdays, stock up to 190.

(For this to be true, day 31 when the month begins would need to be a Saturday, day 30 a Sunday, day 29 a Monday, and so on.)

Finally, what happens to the system as it progresses from one stage to another? Ice-cream sales will vary from day to day and the number

i \ n	31	30	29	28	27	26 . . .
0	200	200	190	190	190	.
1	199	199	189	189	189	.
2	198	198	188	188	188	.
3	197	197	187	187	187	.
4	196	196	186	186	186	.
5	195	195	185	185	185	
6	194	194	184	184	.	
7	193	193	183	.	.	
8	192	192	182	.	.	
9	191	191	181	.	.	
10	190	190	180	.		
11	189	189	179	.		
12	188	188	178	.		
13	187	187	177	.		
.	.	.	.	.		$k_n(i)$
.	.	.	.	.		
.	.	.	.	.		
.	.	.	.	.		
185	15	15	5	.		
186	14	14	4	.		
187	13	13	3	3		
188	12	12	2	2		
189	11	11	1	1		
190	10	10	0	0	.	
191	9	9	0	0	.	
192	8	8	0	0	.	
193	7	7	0	0	.	
194	6	6	0	0	0	
195	5	5	0	0	0	
196	4	4	0	0	0	.
197	3	3	0	0	0	.
198	2	2	0	0	0	.
199	1	1	0	0	0	.
200	0	0	0	0	0	.

Table 1.1

of ice-creams the student has in stock at the beginning of each day will consequently vary. The transformations governing the way in which states change from one stage to another will depend on the structure of the process, which Bellman[4] has classified in 4 levels:

level 0	deterministic
level 1	stochastic (or probabilistic)
level 2	adaptive
level 3 and above	residual

In deterministic processes, an action k in state i at stage n leads to some state j at stage n-1 (the next stage) which we can predict with certainty. In other words, given i and k, j is known. Figure 1.1 may make this more clear, particularly to readers familiar with the concept of state spaces.

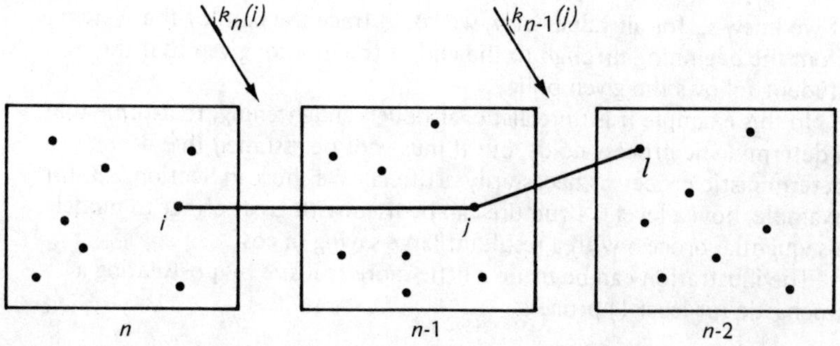

Figure 1.1

The dots in each box represent states which the system could be in at each stage. Initially (at stage n) we are in state i and decision $k_n(i)$ is taken. In consequence, the system makes a transition to state j at the next stage (stage n-1). Given i and $k_n(i)$, then state j is known.

At stage n-1, in state j, another decision is taken: call this decision $k_{n-1}(j)$. In consequence, the system makes a transition to state l at the next stage (stage n-2). Given j and $k_{n-1}(j)$, then state l is known.

All this is for a deterministic process. In the case of the ice-cream seller it is artificial, for if this were a deterministic process we would know how many ice-creams would be sold on each and every day during the month. Nevertheless, suppose we do know this: in particular, we know the demand for ice-creams on the nth day from the end of the month (= s_n, for example). Given i and $k_n(i)$ at stage n, we know j at stage n-1, since

$$j = i + k_n(i) - \min\,(s_n,\ i + k_n(i))$$

or in words

number in stock n-1 days from the end of the month	=	number in stock n days from the end of the month	+	number picked up on the nth day from the end of the month	−	number sold during the nth day from the end of the month

Note that the number sold is governed by both the demand and the stock available. "min $(s_n, i + k_n(i))$" means "whichever is the smaller of s_n and $i + k_n(i)$". If the student uses the given policy, then if he starts at the beginning of the month (n = 31) with 12 ice-creams in stock (i = 12), he will pick up 188 ice-creams and if he sells (say) 60 during his first day

($s_{31} = 60$), then at the beginning of the next day he will have 140 in stock, since

$$140 = 12 + 188 - 60$$

If we knew s_n for all values of n, we could trace the path of the system from the beginning through to the end of the month, given that the student follows the given policy.

In this example it is unrealistic, although enlightening, to assume that a deterministic process holds, but it must not be assumed that a deterministic process is necessarily artificial. We show in Section 2.3, for example, how a level 0 structure can be used with great effect to model a sequential process with a resultant large saving in cost.

The illustration can be made a little more realistic by postulating a stochastic (or level 1) process.

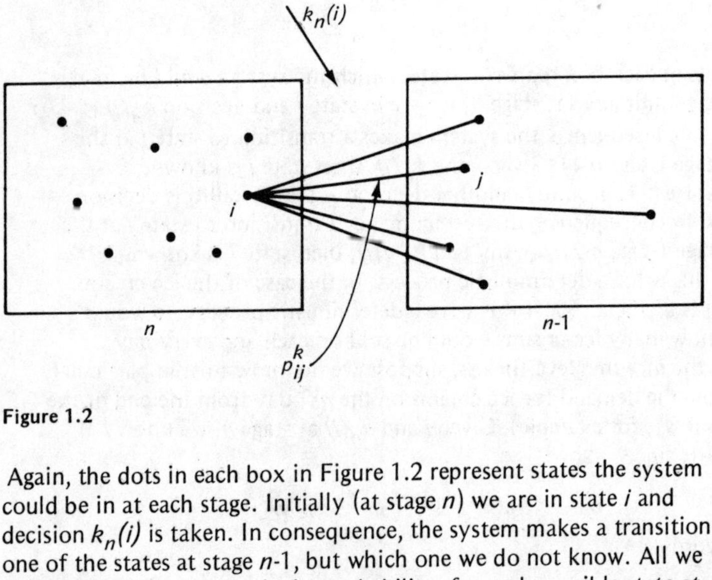

Figure 1.2

Again, the dots in each box in Figure 1.2 represent states the system could be in at each stage. Initially (at stage n) we are in state i and decision $k_n(i)$ is taken. In consequence, the system makes a transition to one of the states at stage n-1, but which one we do not know. All we know in a level 1 process is the probability, for each possible state at the next stage, that that state will be the one the system moves to as a result of being in state i previously and decision $k_n(i)$ having been taken. In other words, given i and $k_n(i)$, then what is known is the probability $p_{ij}^{k_n(i)}$ (or p_{ij}^k in short) of moving from i to j under decision k.

In the case of the ice-cream seller, in a level 1 process, we know the probability distribution of demand for ice-cream on each and every day during the month. That is, we know the probability $p_{s,n}$ (for example) that on the nth day from the end of the month there will be a demand for s ice-creams. To illustrate the nature of transitions in a stochastic process, suppose that on the very first day ($n = 31$) the student has 12 ice-creams in stock, that he follows the given policy and picks up a further 188. Suppose that

with probability $\frac{1}{4}$ there is a demand for 50 ice-creams ($s_{31} = 50$)
with probability $\frac{1}{2}$ there is a demand for 60 ice-creams ($s_{31} = 60$)
with probability $\frac{1}{4}$ there is a demand for 80 ice-creams ($s_{31} = 80$)

We can say then, with the same transition rule as before,

$$j = i + k_n(i) - \min(s_n, i + k_n(i))$$

that

with probability $\frac{1}{4}$, his stock at the beginning of the 30th day from the end of the month will be 150
with probability $\frac{1}{2}$, his stock at the beginning of the 30th day from the end of the month will be 140
with probability $\frac{1}{4}$, his stock at the beginning of the 30th day from the end of the month will be 120.

Notice that in this level 1 process we cannot trace the path of the system from the beginning to the end of the month, since at no stage do we ever know for certain which state will exist at the next stage as a result of taking a specific decision.

Conclusion

In this book we deal, with one exception, only with processes of level 0 and level 1. For the sake of completeness we mention that in the example of the ice-cream seller a level 2 (adaptive) process would be one in which the student learns more about the transition probabilities as the system progresses. For example, he may feel initially that the probability of a demand for 60 ice-creams is $\frac{1}{2}$, but he is prepared to modify his probability assessment according to his experience. If he sells 60 ice-creams each day fairly consistently, then he may raise his probability estimate above $\frac{1}{2}$. Level 3 and above is a catch-all expression: most of the little work done on dynamic processes at this level has been concerned with sequential gaming. In this example it would be as if the student were selling his ice-creams to a competitively minded (and maybe perverse) public and initially knew little, if anything, of the likelihood with which he would sell different numbers of ice-creams. For level 2 processes the reader is referred to White[21]; for level 3 he should consult Bellman.[5, 6]

2
Formulation

2.1 Non-final value systems

Overview

We turn now to some examples of the use of the concepts defined in Chapter 1. In each example we identify the characteristics of the problem: state, decision, transitions, the costs or returns incurred at each stage. We then link them together in the functional equation using the principle of optimality.

In this chapter we deal with two types of system; final value systems and non-final value systems. In final value systems the value of a policy is determined by whether or not a desired final state is reached; in non-final value systems the value of a policy is given by the sum (or the expected sum) of the returns accruing at each stage.

The examples in the following section are of the non-final value type.

Examples

An optimal route Figure 2.1 is a map showing all the routes and distances between any pair of towns, chosen from six towns altogether. In some texts on dynamic programming where a variation of this example is given, the numbers (e.g. the figure 15 between towns 1 and 3) are interpreted

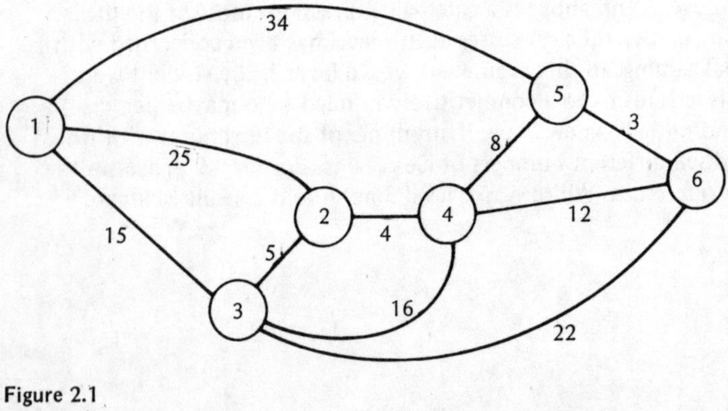

Figure 2.1

as costs: they represent the amounts of protection money to be paid on the various routes to ensure carefree travel, untroubled by brigands. For our purposes either interpretation will serve and we shall work in terms of costs.

We may draw up a table of direct costs *c(i,j)* (Table 2.1), showing the cost of travelling between any pair of towns *i* and *j* in a single step.

from *i* \ to *j*	1	2	3	4	5	6
1	0	25	15	∞	34	∞
2	25	0	5	4	∞	∞
3	15	5	0	16	∞	22
4	∞	4	16	0	8	12
5	34	∞	∞	8	0	3
6	∞	∞	22	12	3	0

Table 2.1

Note that every entry on the diagonal is zero, showing that it costs nothing to go from any town to itself, reasonably enough. Also, the table is symmetrical, so that (for example) it costs the same to go from town 1 to town 3 as it does to go from town 3 to town 1 (15 in either case). Finally, some costs are infinite, showing that there is no direct route between some pairs of towns (like 1 and 4 for instance).

Suppose for some reason we wish to find the least cost route from any town *i* to town 6; not between any pair of towns, only from 1 to 6, 2 to 6, 3 to 6 and so on. Let *f(i)* be the cost of the least cost route from town *i* to town 6. In other words, let *f(i)* be the cost of going from town *i* to town 6 using an optimal policy, where by optimal we mean least cost.

Suppose we are in some town *i* and we want to get to town 6; we need to go directly to some other town and if this other town is not town 6 we want to proceed onwards to town 6 in an optimal manner. Currently we do not know which town we should go to next, but whatever town we do go to next, call it *j*. The cost of going from town *i* to town *j* is *c(i,j)* and the cost of going from town *j* to town 6 using an optimal policy is *f(j)*. Consequently, if from town *i* we go next to town *j* and then proceed optimally thereafter, which is what we ought to do following the principle of optimality, it will cost us

$$c(i,j) + f(j)$$

So far we have not specified *j*; in fact, we can choose *j* (the next town we go to) to be whichever town we want. Our criterion of optimality (as we may call it) is least cost, so we may choose that value of *j* which minimizes $c(i,j) + f(j)$ and write

$$f(i) = \min_{j} [c(i,j) + f(j)],\ i \neq 6$$

$$\text{with } f(6) = 0$$

and we shall use j^* to denote the minimizing value of j.

This equation is true but unhelpful: as it stands it does not enable us to find out what we want to know, since what we want to find out, $f(i)$, also appears on the right-hand side of the equation as one of the $f(j)$. The remedy is to introduce the idea of stages. Suppose we define $f_n(i)$ as the cost of travelling from town i to town 6 using an optimal policy (with optimal meaning least cost, as before) in n steps, where a step is a direct transition from one town to another whose cost is given in the $c(i,j)$ table. Note that we can make a "null" step from town i to town i. We now run through the formulation of the functional equation once more.

Suppose we are in some town i and we want to get to town 6 in n steps. We need to choose some town to go to next; call it j. Going from i to j will cost $c(i,j)$ and uses up a step. Once in town j, we want to proceed optimally in the n-1 steps remaining. Invoking the principle of optimality and remembering that optimal in this example means least cost, we may write

$$f_n(i) = \min_{j} [c(i,j) + f_{n-1}(j)]$$

Now if we knew $f_{n-1}(j)$ for $j = 1, 2, 3, 4, 5$ and 6, we could compute $f_n(i)$ for $i = 1, \ldots, 6$. Knowing $\{f_n(i)\}$ * we could compute $\{f_{n+1}(i)\}$, knowing $\{f_{n+1}(i)\}$ we could compute $\{f_{n+2}(i)\}$, and so on: once we start, we can continue indefinitely. The natural starting point is $\{f_1(i)\}$, since we know that $f_1(i) = c(i,6)$, for the cost of going from any town i to town 6 in one step is $c(i,6)$, the element in the ith row of the last column in the $c(i,j)$ table.

One last point should be noted before the computation. We need only compute $f_n(i)$ for values of n from 1 to 5, since there are only six towns and we shall never need more than five steps. Consider a possible route from town 1, whose first four steps are

$$1 \rightarrow 2 \rightarrow 3 \rightarrow 4 \rightarrow 5$$

(Each arrow represents a step.) On the fifth step the route can only take us to town 6; otherwise a loop will result and since every step which takes us from one town to another costs us something (all the entries in the $c(i,j)$ table for $i \neq j$ are positive), a loop (such as $3 \rightarrow 4 \rightarrow 5 \rightarrow 3$) can never be part of an optimal route. Since an optimal route contains no loops, no town will be visited more than once and the number of steps cannot be more than one less than the number of towns.

*$\{f_n(i)\}$ means "$f_n(i)$ for all i".

We now compute $f_1(i)$, $f_2(i)$ and so on up to $f_5(i)$ for $i = 1$ to 6. Since $f_1(i) = c(i,6)$, we may write $f_1(1) = \infty$, $f_1(2) = \infty$, $f_1(3) = 22$, $f_1(4) = 12$, $f_1(5) = 3$, $f_1(6) = 0$. To help remember the notation, we keep in mind that the number inside the brackets is the number of the town and the suffix represents the number of steps left.

$f_2(1)$ is the cost of travelling from town 1 to town 6 using an optimal policy in 2 steps. From town 1 we may go to any town (j, say) but whichever town j is, from there onwards we must proceed optimally in the remaining steps. Thus if we go from 1 to 3, we must proceed onwards optimally from town 3 in the one step we have left. The same argument holds if we contemplate going to town 5, or town 4, or staying in town 1 or going to any town and we may write

$$f_2(1) = \min_j \left[c(1,j) + f_1(j)\right]$$

or in full

$$f_2(1) = \min \begin{bmatrix} j=1: c(1,1) + f_1(1) \\ j=2: c(1,2) + f_1(2) \\ j=3: c(1,3) + f_1(3) \\ j=4: c(1,4) + f_1(4) \\ j=5: c(1,5) + f_1(5) \\ j=6: c(1,6) + f_1(6) \end{bmatrix}$$

Looking at the right-hand side of this equation we see that all the $c(1,j)$ are known (from the $c(i,j)$ table) and the $f_1(j)$ are known because we have already worked them out, so that

$$f_2(1) = \min \begin{bmatrix} j=1: & 0 + \infty = \infty \\ j=2: & 25 + \infty = \infty \\ j=3: & 15 + 22 = 37 \\ j=4: & \infty + 12 = \infty \\ j=5: & 34 + 3 = 37 \\ j=6: & \infty + 0 = \infty \end{bmatrix}$$

The smallest entries are 37 for $j = 3$ and $j = 5$: therefore we note that if we are in town 1 and we want to go to town 6 in 2 steps, it will cost 37 and the next town to go to is either town 3 or town 5. More formally, we may write

$$f_2(1) = 37$$

$$j_2^*(2) = 3 \text{ or } 5$$

We compute $f_2(2)$ in the same way:

$$f_2(2) = \min \begin{bmatrix} j=1: c(2,1) + f_1(1) \\ j=2: c(2,2) + f_1(2) \\ j=3: c(2,3) + f_1(3) \\ j=4: c(2,4) + f_1(4) \\ j=5: c(2,5) + f_1(5) \\ j=6: c(2,6) + f_1(6) \end{bmatrix} = \min \begin{bmatrix} 25 + \infty = \infty \\ 0 + \infty = \infty \\ 5 + 22 = 27 \\ 4 + 12 = 16 \\ \infty + 3 = \infty \\ \infty + 0 = \infty \end{bmatrix} = 16$$

and we note that $j_2^*(2) = 4$.

Once we have computed $f_2(3)$, $f_2(4)$, and $f_2(5)$ we can compute $f_3(1)$, $f_3(2) \ldots f_3(6)$, then $f_4(1)$, and so on. The complete computation looks like Table 2.2.

$c(i,j)$	i \ j	1	2	3	4	5	6
	1	0	25	15	∞	34	∞
	2	25	0	5	4	∞	∞
	3	15	5	0	16	∞	22
	4	∞	4	16	0	8	12
	5	34	∞	∞	8	0	3
	6	∞	∞	22	12	3	0

i	1	2	3	4	5	6
$f_1(i)$	∞	∞	22	12	3	0
$j_1^*(i)$	6	6	6	6	6	6
$f_2(i)$	37	16	22	11	3	0
$j_2^*(i)$	3 or 5	4	3 or 6	5	5 or 6	6
$f_3(i)$	37	15	21	11	3	0
$j_3^*(i)$	1 or 3 or 5	4	2	4 or 5	5 or 6	6
$f_4(i)$	36	15	20	11	3	0
$j_4^*(i)$	3	2 or 4	2	4 or 5	5 or 6	6
$f_5(i)$	35	15	20	11	3	0
$j_5^*(i)$	3	2 or 4	2 or 3	4 or 5	5 or 6	6

Table 2.2

We now have a schedule of costs and towns to go to next. We can read directly from the $f_5(i)$ row the cost of travelling from any town i to town 6. The least cost route from town 1 to town 6 costs 35, that from town 2 costs 15, and so on. What we need in addition is the actual route to take and we may find this out by a process of backtracking.

Remember that $f_n(i)$ is the cost of going from town i to town 6 using an optimal policy in at most n steps, and $j_n{}^*(i)$ is the town to go to next using that optimal policy. Consequently if we are in town 1 and want to get to town 6 in at most 5 steps, it will cost us 35 and the next town to go to is town 3. Going to town 3 uses up a step, so when we are in town 3 we shall want to get to town 6 in at most 4 steps; in short we are interested in $f_4(3)$ and $j_4{}^*(3)$. We see from the table that $f_4(3) = 20$ and $j_4{}^*(3) = 2$: that is, the next town to go to is town 2. This will use up another step, so that when we are in town 2 we shall want to go to town 6 in at most 3 steps. The next results to be read are $f_3(2) = 15$ and $j_3{}^*(2) = 4$; therefore the next town to go to is town 4. From town 4 we go to town 5 (since $j_2{}^*(4) = 5$) and from town 5, not surprisingly, since now we have only 1 step left, we go to town 6 ($j_1{}^*(5) = 6$).

We may summarize the backtracking process from town 1 as

n:	5		4		3		2		1		
i:	1	→	3	→	2	→	4	→	5	→	6
$f_n(i)$:	35		20		15		11		3		
$c(i,j_n{}^*(i))$:		15		5		4		8		3	

Note how the $\{f_n(i)\}$ are built up cumulatively from the successive single-step costs:

$$f_2(4) = c(4,5) + f_1(5)$$
$$\text{or } 11 = 8 + 3$$

$$f_3(2) = c(2,4) + f_2(4)$$
$$\text{or } 15 = 4 + 11$$

$$f_4(3) = c(3,2) + f_3(2)$$
$$\text{or } 20 = 5 + 15$$

and finally

$$f_5(1) = c(1,3) + f_4(3)$$
$$\text{or } 35 = 15 + 20$$

and of course

$$\begin{aligned} f_5(1) &= c(1,3) + c(3,2) + c(2,4) + c(4,5) + c(5,6) \\ &= 15 + 5 + 4 + 8 + 3 \\ &= 35 \end{aligned}$$

It is instructive to backtrack from various places in the computation and the reader may be interested in verifying the backtracking this time from town 2. (See Table 2.3.)

i	1	2	3	4	5	6
$f_1(i)$	∞	∞	22	12	3	0
$j_1{}^*(i)$	6	6	6	6	6	6
$f_2(i)$	37	16	22	11	3	0
$j_2{}^*(i)$	3 or 5	4	3 or 6	5	5 or 6	6
$f_3(i)$	37	15	21	11	3	0
$j_3{}^*(i)$	1 or 3 or 5	4	2	4 or 5	5 or 6	6
$f_4(i)$	36	15	20	11	3	0
$j_4{}^*(i)$	3	2 or 4	2	4 or 5	5 or 6	6
$f_5(i)$	35	15	20	11	3	0
$j_5{}^*(i)$	3	2 or 4	2 or 3	4 or 5	5 or 6	6

Table 2.3

There appear to be a number of alternative optimal routes, but if we write them all down we see that this is not so:

$$
\begin{array}{l}
2 \to 2 \to 2 \to 4 \to 5 \to 6 \\
2 \to 2 \to 4 \to 4 \to 5 \to 6 \\
2 \to 2 \to 4 \to 5 \to 5 \to 6 \\
2 \to 2 \to 4 \to 5 \to 6 \to 6 \\
2 \to 4 \to 4 \to 4 \to 5 \to 6 \\
2 \to 4 \to 4 \to 5 \to 5 \to 6 \\
2 \to 4 \to 4 \to 5 \to 6 \to 6 \\
2 \to 4 \to 5 \to 5 \to 5 \to 6 \\
2 \to 4 \to 5 \to 5 \to 6 \to 6 \\
2 \to 4 \to 5 \to 6 \to 6 \to 6
\end{array}
$$

All the routes given above are simply the 5-step variants of the optimal route

$$2 \to 4 \to 5 \to 6$$

when three steps are all we need. This may be seen from the Table 2.3 computations, since $f_3(2)$ is the same as $f_4(2)$ which is the same as $f_5(2)$. The sequence $f_n(2)$ stops decreasing after $f_3(2)$.

We can also see from the table that 4 steps are all we need to go from town 3 to town 6 at minimal cost, 2 steps from town 4 and 1 step from town 5. For a given town i, $f_n(i)$ is monotonic decreasing in n; or in other words, as n increases $f_n(i)$ either stays the same or decreases. This is illustrated by Figure 2.2.

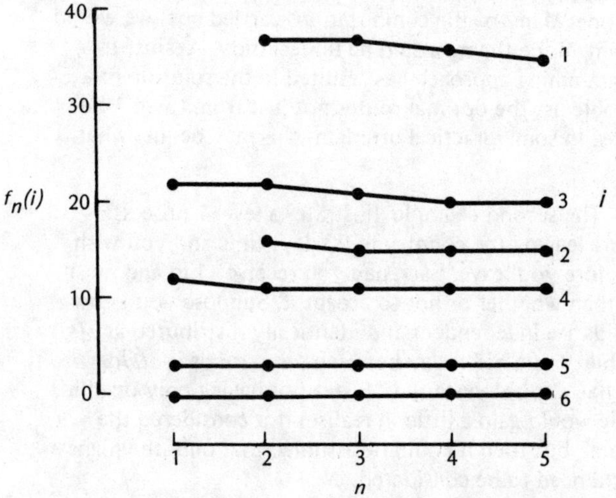

Figure 2.2

If the computation were continued after $n = 5$, we would find that $f_6(i)$ and $j_6{}^*(i)$ were

i	1	2	3	4	5	6
$f_6(i)$	35	15	20	11	3	0
$j_6{}^*(i)$	1 or 3	2 or 4	2 or 3	4 or 5	5 or 6	6

and these entries would be repeated over and over again. The sequence $f_n(i)$ has settled down and what we now have is effectively a solution to the original equation (the one without the steps):

$$f(i) = \min_j \left[c(i,j) + f(j)\right]$$

and we could derive the optimal route from the j^* row:

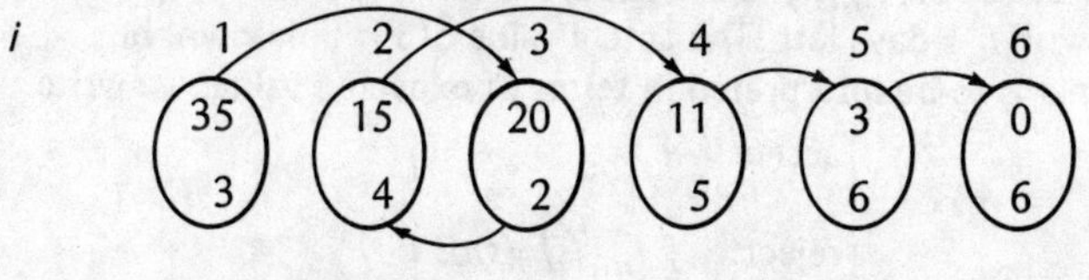

Note that the alternative j^* have been dropped. If we went from town 1 to town 1 we would always stay in town 1 and never get to town 6; consequently, we must go to some town j other than i.

Finally, we raise the issue of redundancy in computation. Suppose we wanted to find the optimal route only from town 1 to town 6. In this event we would still have had to compute $f_1(i)$, $f_2(i)$, . . . $f_4(i)$ for all i, and then $f_5(1)$ alone. Many of the computations carried out (we would find out after having done them) would be unnecessary. Against this, the dynamic programming approach has resulted in the solution of a whole class of problems: the optimal routes not just from town 1 but from all the towns. In some practical problems this may be just what is needed.

Selling a car The second example illustrates a level 1 process.

Suppose you are leaving the country in 20 days time and you wish to sell your car before you leave. Each day you receive a bid and must decide there and then whether or not to accept it. Suppose you know that these daily bids are independent and identically distributed as $\phi(s)$: that is, the probability of a bid today between s and $s + ds$ is $\phi(s)ds$, independent of what was bid yesterday. Instead of having only one bid a day, the example would gain a little in realism if it considered the possibility of several, but then it could be assumed that only the highest bid each day would need to be considered.

The formulation of the problem in dynamic programming terms is straightforward. Each day (stage) you receive a bid x (state) and you have to decide whether or not to accept it (decision). All that is left is the criterion of optimality and, for simplicity, we take this as maximizing expected revenue (in the mathematical sense of expectation). Adopting this criterion, we may define $f_n(x)$ as the expected value of just having had a bid of x, with n days left to the time horizon (when you are due to leave the country), using an optimal policy where optimal means maximal expected revenue.

If you accept the bid of x, then it is pointless thinking about bids you may be offered afterwards if you do not accept it: you sell the car and receive x, which is the actual revenue resulting from the decision taken. If you do not accept the bid, then tomorrow you will be in a similar situation, one day nearer the time horizon, with just having had a bid s (for instance) and whatever s is, you will want to proceed optimally. But the expected value of proceeding optimally, if you have just had a bid of s, with n-1 days left to the time horizon, is $f_{n-1}(s)$. Whatever value s has, $f_{n-1}(s)$ is the expected value of proceeding optimally with n-1 days left. The actual value of s is unknown, but since optimal is to be interpreted in terms of expected value, we write

$$f_n(x) = \max \begin{bmatrix} \text{accept:} & x \\ \text{reject:} & \int_0^\infty f_{n-1}(s)\phi(s)ds \end{bmatrix} \qquad n \geqslant 1$$

Now consider the scene on the day of your departure when, if you have not already accepted an offer, you receive your last bid. There is nothing for it but to accept it, however low it is and we write

$$f_0(x) = x$$

Knowing $f_0(x)$ for all values of x, we can compute $f_1(x)$ for all values of x, then $f_2(x)$, . . . and finally $f_{19}(x)$ for all values of x. Thus

$$f_1(x) = \max \begin{bmatrix} \text{accept: } x \\ \text{reject: } \int_0^\infty f_0(s)\phi(s)ds \end{bmatrix}$$

$$= \max \begin{bmatrix} x \\ \int_0^\infty s\phi(s)ds \end{bmatrix}$$

$$= \max \begin{bmatrix} x \\ \mu \end{bmatrix}, \text{ where } \mu = \int_0^\infty s\phi(s)ds$$

so that with one day left, you should accept a bid if and only if it is greater than the mean value of the probability distribution of bids.

The optimal policy is to accept a bid, with n days left, if and only if it is greater than some critical value λ_n; when the bid is equal to λ_n it does not matter whether it is accepted or rejected. We can show this inductively. Suppose

$$f_n(x) = \max \begin{bmatrix} x \\ \lambda_n \end{bmatrix}$$

then

$$f_{n+1}(x) = \max \begin{bmatrix} \text{accept: } x \\ \text{reject: } \int_0^\infty f_n(s)\phi(s)ds \end{bmatrix}$$

$$= \max \begin{bmatrix} x \\ \int_0^{\lambda_n} f_n(s)\phi(s)ds + \int_{\lambda_n}^\infty f_n(s)\phi(s)ds \end{bmatrix}$$

$$= \max \begin{bmatrix} x \\ \lambda_n \int_0^{\lambda_n} \phi(s)ds + \int_{\lambda_n}^\infty s\phi(s)ds \end{bmatrix}$$

$$= \max \begin{bmatrix} x \\ \lambda_{n+1} \end{bmatrix}$$

where $\lambda_{n+1} = \lambda_n \int_0^{\lambda_n} \phi(s)ds + \int_{\lambda_n}^\infty s\phi(s)ds$

What has been done here is to split the integral between 0 and λ_n and between λ_n and ∞, and then to note that

$$\text{for } s \leqslant \lambda_n,\ f_n(s) = \lambda_n$$
$$\text{for } s \geqslant \lambda_n,\ f_n(s) = s$$

Mathematically inclined readers may be interested in verifying that if $\phi(s)$ is uniformly distributed between 0 and 2μ, then

$$\lambda_{n+1} = \mu + \frac{\lambda_n^{\;2}}{4\mu}, \text{ with } \lambda_0 = 0$$

Readers not so mathematically inclined may prefer a numerical example. Suppose that the daily distribution of bids is

£	*Probability* p_s
200	0.5
300	0.2
400	0.2
500	0.1

With an obvious modification to the previous example in which the probability distribution of bids was continuous and not discrete, we may write

$$f_n(x) = \max \begin{bmatrix} \text{accept:} & x \\ \text{reject:} & \sum_s f_{n-1}(s)p_s \end{bmatrix} \qquad n \geqslant 1$$

and as before $f_0(x) = x$.

$$\text{Thus } f_1(x) = \max \begin{bmatrix} x \\ 0.5f_0(200) + 0.2f_0(300) + 0.2f_0(400) \\ + 0.1f_0(500) \end{bmatrix}$$

$$= \max \begin{bmatrix} x \\ 0.5 \times 200 + 0.2 \times 300 + 0.2 \times 400 + 0.1 \times 500 \end{bmatrix}$$

$$= \max \begin{bmatrix} x \\ 290 \end{bmatrix}$$

and with one day left you should accept the bid if and only if it is greater than £290, i.e. if you have a bid of £300, £400 or £500. We may construct Table 2.4.

x	$f_1(x)$	Decision
200	290	reject
300	300	accept
400	400	accept
500	500	accept

Table 2.4

$$\text{Also } f_2(x) = \max \begin{bmatrix} x \\ 0.5f_1(200) + 0.2f_1(300) + 0.2f_1(400) + 0.1f_1(500) \end{bmatrix}$$

$$= \max \begin{bmatrix} x \\ 0.5 \times 290 + 0.2 \times 300 + 0.2 \times 400 + 0.1 \times 500 \end{bmatrix}$$

$$= \max \begin{bmatrix} x \\ 335 \end{bmatrix}$$

so that with two days left you should accept the bid if and only if it is greater than £335, i.e. if you have a bid of £400 or £500. Table 2.5 is the corresponding table.

x	$f_2(x)$	Decision
200	335	reject
300	335	reject
400	400	accept
500	500	accept

Table 2.5

So far we have computed $\lambda_1 = 290$ and $\lambda_2 = 335$. In a similar way, we could compute successive values of λ_n thus:

$$\lambda_3 = 0.5 \times 335 + 0.2 \times 335 + 0.2 \times 400 + 0.1 \times 500$$
$$= 364.5$$

$$\lambda_4 = 0.5 \times 364.5 + 0.2 \times 364.5 + 0.2 \times 400 + 0.1 \times 500$$
$$= 385.15$$

$$\lambda_5 = 0.5 \times 385.15 + 0.2 \times 385.15 + 0.2 \times 400 + 0.1 \times 500$$
$$= 400.505$$

Consequently, with five days left you should accept only a £500 bid, and since λ_n increases with n (the longer there is until your departure date) this also holds when there are more than five days left. Thus the optimal policy may be shown as Table 2.6.

x \ n	0	1	2	3	4	5 or more
200	accept	reject	reject	reject	reject	reject
300	accept	accept	reject	reject	reject	reject
400	accept	accept	accept	accept	accept	reject
500	accept	accept	accept	accept	accept	accept

Table 2.6

Note that, as always, the policy tells you what action to take according to the state you are in and the stage you are at.

Finally we see that (as in the optimal route example) although we were able to compute the $f_n(.)$* successively, in this example there is no question of backtracking: backtracking is meaningful only in deterministic systems. In a stochastic process we cannot predict precisely what is going to happen and we cannot know beforehand which state the system will be in at any stage; what we can do is work out the policy which will tell us the best action to take at each stage, whatever state the system is in.

The knapsack problem The third example is one of a class of problems generally known as allocation problems, in which the objective is to maximize an objective function subject to one or more constraints. Practical examples are the allocation of an advertising budget among alternative promotional campaigns, or the allocation of a research and development budget among possible projects. If both constraints and objective function are linear, then such problems can be treated as linear programming problems, but when the constraints and objective function are non-linear, linear programming cannot be used unless some approximations are made.

A well-known type of allocation problem is the so-called knapsack problem in which it is required to employ a resource in various ways so as to maximize the return on its use. Presumably the name knapsack has arisen from the problem a hiker has in filling his knapsack with the various items which he would like to take with him, subject to a limit on the weight he is prepared to carry around on his back: the hiker's objective is to maximize the total value to him of the items he carries.

* $f_n(.)$ is a general form; it means "$f_n(\ )$ for all values of the argument" or in this instance "$f_n(x)$ for all x".

More formally, suppose there are N items (which are candidates for the knapsack) and each of the items has a value given by some function: specifically, let x_n units of the nth item have a value of $v_n(x_n)$. Clearly v_n may well be non-linear: two blankets may be twice as good as one but probably three blankets will not be three times as good, so that in this case $v(2) = 2v(1)$ but $v(3) < 3v(1)$. Suppose a unit of the nth item weighs w_n and the maximal allowable weight for the contents of the knapsack is C. Then we may write the problem in this form:

$$\text{maximize} \sum_{n=1}^{N} v_n(x_n) \text{ subject to}$$

$$\sum_{n=1}^{N} w_n x_n = C, x_n \geqslant 0$$

One way of tackling a problem expressed in this way is to use Lagrange multipliers and to consider the derived objective function

$$\text{maximize} \sum_{n=1}^{N} v_n(x_n) - \lambda \left(\sum_{n=1}^{N} w_n x_n - C \right)$$

Differentiating this equation with respect to each of the x_n in turn and equating to zero would result in the N equations

$$v'_n(x_n) - \lambda w_n = 0$$

and together with the requirement

$$\sum_{n=1}^{N} w_n x_n = C$$

there would result $N + 1$ equations from which the unknown optimal values of the N x_n and λ could in principle be determined. Alternatively, we might choose some value of λ, solve the N equations

$$v'_n(x_n) - \lambda w_n = 0$$

and repeat this procedure until we hit on a value of λ which is such that

$$\sum_{n=1}^{N} w_n x_n = C$$

There are several computational drawbacks to such a procedure. Firstly, it may not be possible to differentiate the v_n. Secondly, some of the optimal values of the x_n may turn out to be negative, whereas only positive or zero values are required. Thirdly, the x_n may need to satisfy some requirements of discreteness: for instance, the x_n may all have to be integers. Any one of these reasons reduces the applicability of Lagrange multipliers and motivates an approach through dynamic programming.

To establish these ideas we consider the problem of loading a barge with cargo comprising packages of four types ($N = 4$). The maximal weight of cargo which the barge can carry is 100 tons ($C = 100$). Each package of the nth type has a value v_n and a weight w_n as follows:

Package type (n)	*Weight (tons) per package (w_n)*	*Value per package (v_n)*
1	40	42
2	30	26
3	15	11
4	8	7

The object of the exercise is to load the barge with that combination of packages of types 1 to 4 which has maximal value while weighing not more than 100 tons. Formally, the problem is identical with the knapsack problem.

As posed, this does not appear to be a sequential problem and the applicability of dynamic programming is not immediately obvious. A narrative may help. Imagine loading the barge first with packages of type 4, then with packages of type 3, then with packages of type 2 and lastly packages of type 1. Until the time comes to load packages of type n, we shall not know how much tonnage (technically called ullage) there will be available for loading packages of types 1 to n, so let it be W. We may now define $f_n(W)$ as the value associated with having an ullage of W tons, with packages of types 1 to n available for loading, using an optimal policy. In this example optimal means greatest value.

The functional equation can now be derived. If we load x_n packages of type n, the value of packages carried by the barge will increase by $x_n v_n$ and the ullage available for loading with packages of the first $n-1$ types will decrease from W to $W - x_n w_n$. We shall wish to use this ullage optimally and therefore write

$$f_n(W) = \max_{0 \leqslant x_n \leqslant \left[\frac{W}{w_n}\right]} \left(x_n v_n + f_{n\text{-}1}(W - x_n w_n)\right) \quad , n \geqslant 2$$

Notice that x_n, the number of packages of the nth type, must be greater than or equal to zero (obviously) but that the weight of the x_n packages cannot be greater than the weight W available for loading, so that

$$x_n w_n \leqslant W$$

and
$$x_n \leqslant \left[\frac{W}{w_n}\right]$$

where $\left[\frac{W}{w_n}\right]$ signifies the largest integer not exceeding $\frac{W}{w_n}$.

When we eventually come to load packages of the first type, we can load up the barge with as much as it can carry and consequently

$$f_1(W) = \max_{0 \leqslant x_1 \leqslant \left[\frac{W}{w_1}\right]} (x_1 v_1)$$

By successively evaluating the $f_n(.)$ Table 2.7 may be derived:

W	$f_1(W)$	$x_1{}^*(W)$	$f_2(W)$	$x_2{}^*(W)$	$f_3(W)$	$x_3{}^*(W)$	$f_4(W)$	$x_4{}^*(W)$
100	84	2	94	2	95	1	98	2
95	84	2	84	0	95	1		
90	84	2	84	0	84	0		
85	84	2	84	0	84	0		
80	84	2	84	0	84	0		
75	42	1	68	1	68	0		
70	42	1	68	1	68	0		
65	42	1	52	2	53	1		
60	42	1	52	2	53	1		
55	42	1	42	0	53	1		
50	42	1	42	0	42	0		
45	42	1	42	0	42	0		
40	42	1	42	0	42	0		
35	0	0	26	1	26	0		
30	0	0	26	1	26	0		
25	0	0	0	0	11	1		
20	0	0	0	0	11	1		
15	0	0	0	0	11	1		
10	0	0	0	0	0	0		
5	0	0	0	0	0	0		

Table 2.7

This is a level 0 problem and, as with the optimal route example on p. 10, we compute the successive $f_n(W)$ and at each state make a note of the optimizing decision, in this case $x_n{}^*(W)$. There are two points of interest in the computation.

Firstly, we do not need to consider loading more than two packages of type 2, since three packages would weigh 90 tons and have a value of 78, whereas two packages of type 1 weigh less and are worth more (80 tons, 84). A similar argument shows that $x_3{}^* \leqslant 1$, and $x_4{}^* \leqslant 4$. We would not get a different answer if we did not realise that the upper limits on x_3 and x_4 set by $\left[\frac{W}{w_3}\right]$ and $\left[\frac{W}{w_4}\right]$ could be improved, but we would have carried out additional computation needlessly. It never hurts to think hard about problem simplification before starting the computation.

Secondly, we do not need to compute $f_n(W)$ for all values of W, since there is only one package (package 4) whose weight is not a multiple of 5 tons. Thus in computing $f_4(100)$ we write

$$f_4(100) = \max \begin{bmatrix} x_4 = 0: & 0 + f_3(100) \\ x_4 = 1: & 7 + f_3(92) \\ x_4 = 2: & 14 + f_3(84) \\ x_4 = 3: & 21 + f_3(76) \\ x_4 = 4: & 28 + f_3(68) \end{bmatrix}$$

$$= \max \begin{bmatrix} 0 + f_3(100) \\ 7 + f_3(90) \\ 14 + f_3(80) \\ 21 + f_3(75) \\ 18 + f_3(65) \end{bmatrix}$$

$$= \max \begin{bmatrix} 0 + 95 \\ 7 + 84 \\ 14 + 84 \\ 21 + 68 \\ 28 + 53 \end{bmatrix}$$

$$= \max \begin{bmatrix} 95 \\ 91 \\ 98 \\ 89 \\ 81 \end{bmatrix}$$

$$= 98, \text{ and } x_4^* = 2$$

To find the optimal loading policy we backtrack as usual in level 0 problems and we show this as

n	4	3	2	1
x_n^*:	2	0	0	2
W:	100 →	84=80 →	80 →	80
$f_n(W)$:	98	84	84	84
$v_n(x_n^*)$:	14	0	0	84

In words, we load two packages each of types 1 and 4 for a total value of 98.

It is worthwhile finding $f_4(W)$ and $x_4{}^*(W)$ for other values of W besides $W = 100$, to show the way in which dynamic programming can give the solution to a whole class of problems with very little extra computational effort. This is done in Table 2.8, in which, for the sake of illustration, the backtracking has been marked for $f_4(100)$, $f_4(75)$ and $f_4(50)$.

W	$f_1(W)$	$x_1{}^*(W)$	$f_2(W)$	$x_2{}^*(W)$	$f_3(W)$	$x_3{}^*(W)$	$f_4(W)$	$x_4{}^*(W)$
100	84	2	94	2	95	1	98	2
95	84	2	84	0	95	1	95	0
90	84	2	84	0	84	0	91	1
85	84	2	84	0	84	0	84	0
80	84	2	84	0	84	0	84	0
75	42	1	68	1	68	0	70	4
70	42	1	68	1	68	0	68	0
65	42	1	52	2	53	1	63	3
60	42	1	52	2	53	1	56	2
55	42	1	42	0	53	1	53	0
50	42	1	42	0	42	0	49	1
45	42	1	42	0	42	0	42	0
40	42	1	42	0	42	0	42	0
35	0	0	26	1	26	0	28	4
30	0	0	26	1	26	0	26	0
25	0	0	0	0	11	1	21	3
20	0	0	0	0	11	1	14	2
15	0	0	0	0	11	1	11	0
10	0	0	0	0	0	0	7	1
5	0	0	0	0	0	0	0	0

Table 2.8

It is easy to verify two obvious points from Table 2.8, namely

$$f_{n+1}(W) \geqslant f_n(W),$$

$$\text{and} \quad f_n(W_1) \geqslant f_n(W_2) \text{ if } W_1 > W_2$$

The first inequality makes the point that we are at least as well off if we can fill the barge with the first $n + 1$ types of packages instead of only the first n, and the second that we are at least as well off if we have more ullage available for loading. They are algebraic statements of what follows from commonsense.

Finally, a point must be mentioned about the ordering of the package types. If all we want to do is find the optimal combination of packages using dynamic programming and we do not care how long it takes us to find it, then there is no reason for our ordering the package types in one way rather than another. It will have been noticed that they are in fact ranged more or less in descending order of value per unit weight. If we had ordered the packages in reverse, i.e. the former number 4 becoming number 1 and so on, then in computing $f_1(W)$ for all values of W in the new ordering we would have to consider possible values of x_1 from 0 to 12, thirteen possibilities in all, since it is possible to load up to twelve 8-ton packages with a 100-ton ullage.

Similarly in computing $f_2(W)$ for all values of W, we would have to consider values of x_2 from 0 to 6, and in computing $f_3(W)$ for all values of W, values of x_3 from 0 to 3.

Table 2.9 is the complete table of cargo values and associated decisions. The $f_4(W)$ values in this table are of course identical to those

W	$f_1(W)$	$x_1^*(W)$	$f_2(W)$	$x_2^*(W)$	$f_3(W)$	$x_3^*(W)$	$f_4(W)$	$x_4^*(W)$
100	84	12	84	0	87	2	98	2
95	77	11	81	1	82	1	95	2
90	77	11	77	0	78	3	91	2
85	70	10	70	0	73	2	84	2
80	70	10	70	0	70	0	84	2
75	63	9	60	1	63	2	70	1
70	56	8	57	2	61	1	68	1
65	56	8	56	0	56	0	63	1
60	49	7	49	0	52	2	56	1
55	42	6	46	1	47	1	53	1
50	42	6	42	0	42	0	49	1
45	35	5	35	0	37	1	42	1
40	35	5	35	0	35	0	42	1
35	28	4	28	0	28	0	28	0
30	21	3	22	2	26	1	26	0
25	21	3	21	0	21	0	21	0
20	14	2	14	0	14	0	14	0
15	7	1	11	1	11	0	11	0
10	7	1	7	0	7	0	7	0
5	0	0	0	0	0	0	0	0

Table 2.9

in the previous one; for interest, the backtracking from $f_4(100)$, $f_4(75)$ and $f_4(50)$ is marked.

Conclusion

With the experience of these three examples, we may lay down guidelines on formulation.

Problem characteristics

Problem	State	Decision	Single-stage costs or returns	Transitions
Optimal	*i:* town we are in	*j:* town to go to next	$c(i,j)$	$j(i) = j$: if you decide to go to town j next, town j is where you go (level 0)
Selling a car	*x:* bid just received	accept	x	process terminates
		or reject	0	$x \to s$ where s is a random variable with probability distribution $\phi(s)$: s is tomorrow's bid whose probability distribution is known (level 1)
Loading the barge	*W:* ullage available for loading	x_n: how many packages of type n to load	$x_n v_n$: each package of type n is worth v_n	$W \to W - x_n w_n$: each package of type n loaded reduces the ullage by w_n (level 0)

Criteria of optimality

Problem	Objective
Optimal route	minimize cost
Selling a car	maximize expected revenue
Loading the barge	maximize total value

Start of computation

Problem	Start of computation
Optimal route	$f_1(i) = c(i,6)$: cost of going from town i to town 6 in one step
Selling a car	$f_0(x) = x$: we have to accept the very last bid
Loading the barge	$f_1(W) = \max_{0 \leqslant x_1 w_1 \leqslant W} (x_1 v_1)$: we load as many type 1 packages as we can

Figure 2.3

We first identify the characteristics of the problem:

state
decisions
single-stage costs or returns
transitions

and then we specify the criterion of optimality, or the objective. Having done so, we formulate the functional equation; finally, the computation is started. We can now summarize (in Figure 2.3) how these three steps were carried out for the problems formulated in this chapter.

In practice, it may be difficult to follow these guidelines, especially in identifying problem characteristics, since the state description in particular is often very complicated. Nevertheless, when one is faced with a problem which it is thought may be amenable to a dynamic programming approach, the guidelines will usually lead to an appropriate formulation if one is possible.

2.2 Final Value Systems

Overview

Identifying the states, decisions, returns and transitions is only one part of the formulation process: the other part is to define the objective. In the preceding examples this was straightforward: this section discusses two examples where the criterion of optimality may give rise to some conceptual difficulties.

In the preceding examples the criterion of optimality was to maximize total revenue (or expected revenue) or to minimize total costs, this total being the sum of returns or costs incurred at each stage. In the two following examples the criterion of optimality is concerned with maximizing the probability of reaching a given state. Systems which have this criterion of optimality are known as final value systems.

Examples

A pattern of search As the first illustration, consider a situation where we need to find a person or an object whose location is uncertain within a general area and must maximize the probability of finding the person or object within a fixed time. In wartime it may be required to locate quickly the position of an enemy submarine; in peacetime it may be required to rescue a hill-walker who is known to have only enough food to keep himself alive for a certain number of days.

To use a specific example, consider a missing walker who is known to be in one of s areas, numbered 1 to s, and suppose it is thought that the probability that he is in area i is p_i, and that if he is in area i and we look for him there, then the probability with which we will find him is q_i. Finally, suppose that it takes a time t_i to search area i.

In this case it is straightforward to identify the problem characteristics. The state is the vector of probabilities $(p_1, p_2 \ldots p_s)$ that the walker will be in area i together with the amount of time there is left; the decision is which area to search next; there are no single stage costs; the transitions can be worked out simply using Bayes's theorem.[11] If we decide to search area k next, then

either we find the missing walker with probability $p_k q_k$

or we do not find him with probability $1 - p_k q_k$

and in the next state we will have to decide which area to search next with revised probabilities $p'_{k1}, p'_{k2}, \ldots p'_{ks}$.

We recall that Bayes's theorem may be expressed in the form

$$P(B/A) = \frac{P(A/B)P(B)}{P(A/B)P(B) + P(A/C)P(C)}$$

where A may be regarded as some event and B and C as two exclusive and exhaustive hypotheses. In the present case A is the event: we look for the walker in area k and do not find him, and B and C are respectively the hypotheses that the walker is and is not in area k. Thus $P(B/A)$ denotes the probability that the walker is in area k if we have searched area k and not found him.

Clearly $P(A/C)$, the probability that we look for the walker in area k and do not find him if he is not there anyway, is equal to one and we may write

$$p'_{kk} = \frac{(1-q_k)p_k}{(1-q_k)p_k + 1(1-p_k)}$$

$$= \frac{(1-q_k)p_k}{1-q_k p_k}$$

It is easy to show that the revised probability that the walker is in area j $(j \neq k)$, given that we have just searched area k and not found him, is

$$p'_{kj} = \frac{p_j}{1-q_k p_k}$$

Thus defining $f(T: p_1, p_2, p_3 \ldots p_s)$ as the probability of finding the missing walker in the next T time units, with probability p_1 that he is in area 1, and so on, using an optimal policy where optimal means maximizing the probability of finding the walker, we may write for values of $T \geqslant 0$

$$f(T; p_1, p_2, \ldots p_s) = \max_{k: t \leqslant T} \left[p_k q_k + (1-p_k q_k) f(T-t_k : p'_{k1}, p'_{k2} \ldots p'_{ks}) \right]$$

with $p'_{k1}, \ldots p'_{ks}$ already defined.

The functional equation is relatively easy to establish, but the optimal policy may be difficult to compute in a particular case because of the high dimensionality of the state description in which there are $s + 1$ variables. We shall deal with questions of computation in Chapter 4.

Choosing a secretary In Section 2.1 (p. 18) we considered the problem of selling a car when the daily bids were distributed identically and independently according to a known probability density function. Mathematically inclined readers were invited to verify that the critical levels λ_{n+1} were given by $\lambda_{n+1} = \frac{\lambda_n{}^2}{4\mu} + \mu$, with $\lambda_0 = 0$ (when there were $n + 1$ days left bids below λ_{n+1} should not be accepted, and where bids were uniformly distributed between 0 and 2μ). It is a trivial exercise to show that the same dynamic programming formulation holds if we consider how to choose a secretary in an optimal manner when we interview candidates for the position successively. As soon as we choose a candidate, the ones remaining to be interviewed may be sent home, since we are not allowed to change our mind once we have accepted a candidate and if we reject a candidate at the time we interview her, we cannot change our mind and bring her back. Thus if it were possible to give candidates a mark (out of 100, for example), then we might wish to follow a policy which would maximize the expected mark of the candidate selected. If the marks of candidates are independently and identically distributed according to a uniform distribution between 0 and 100, a little arithmetic will yield the critical levels

$$\lambda_0 = 0$$
$$\lambda_1 = 50$$
$$\lambda_2 = 62.5$$
$$\lambda_3 = 69.53125$$

so that (to the nearest integer) out of four candidates, we could accept the first if she scores 70 or more, the second if she scores 63 or more and we have not already accepted the first, and the third if she scores 50 or more and we have not accepted either of the first two. We assume as before that one of the candidates must be accepted.

Suppose, however, that our criterion is not to maximize the expected mark of the chosen candidate, but to maximize the probability of choosing the best candidate. This objective makes the problem much more difficult. In identifying the problem characteristics, we note that the stages and the decisions are as before, but the state description requires an extra dimension. We may imagine ourselves interviewing a candidate, with n more candidates still to be interviewed and the current candidate having a mark x. Unless x is the highest mark of any candidate seen so far, there is no point in choosing this one; if we do, the probability of choosing the best candidate is zero. Consequently, we need to record in the state description the value of the highest mark awarded so far. As an initial formulation to be justified later, we therefore define $f_n(a,x)$ as the probability of selecting the best candidate, with n more candidates still to interview, with the best candidate so far having had a mark a, and with the present candidate having a mark x, using an optimal policy. In this case optimal signifies maximizing the probability of choosing the candidate with the highest mark. For convenience, we consider a uniform distribution of marks between 0 and 1, rather than between 0 and 100. We may write

$$f_n(a,x) = \begin{bmatrix} x < a: \int_0^1 f_{n-1}(a,s)ds \\ x \geqslant a: \max \begin{Bmatrix} \text{accept } x^n \\ \text{reject } \int_0^1 f_{n-1}(x,s)ds \end{Bmatrix} \end{bmatrix}$$

and

$$f_0(a,x) = 1, x \geqslant a$$
$$= 0, x < a$$

Starting the computation is easy: if and when we interview the last candidate, either she is the best $(x \geqslant a)$ in which case we choose the best candidate with probability one, or she is not the best $(x < a)$ in which case we choose the best with probability zero. With n candidates still to be interviewed, we have a real choice only if the current candidate is the best so far $(x \geqslant a)$. If we reject her, we shall henceforth proceed optimally starting with the first of the remaining n candidates, who will have some mark between s and s + ds with probability $\phi(s)$ds say, where $\phi(s) = 1$ over the range (0,1). The best mark so far, if we reject the current candidate, will then be x (the current candidate's mark) and the probability of choosing the best candidate will then be $\int_0^1 f_{n-1}(x,s)ds$, as there will then be $n-1$ candidates still to be interviewed. If we accept her, the probability that she is in fact the best candidate is the probability that each of the remaining n candidates would be given a mark lower than x; since these n events are independent, this probability is equal to x^n.

This formulation is not strictly a final value system since it is impossible to specify the target state. At any terminal state we shall be in a state (a,x), where a may refer to a subset of stages the rest of which we shall never know. For a formulation appropriate to a final value system, we need to introduce a third variable into the state description. We must define $f_n(a,x,h)$ as the probability of choosing the best candidate, with n more candidates still to interview, with the best candidate so far having had a mark a, with the present candidate having a mark x, using an optimal policy, with h having the following interpretation:

$h = 0$	no candidate accepted so far
$h = 1$	a candidate accepted, with a mark of a
$h = 2$	a candidate accepted, with a mark below a

We may now write

$$f_n(a,x,2) = \int_0^1 f_{n-1}(\max(a,x),s,2)ds$$

$$f_n(a,x,1) = \begin{bmatrix} x < a: & \int_0^1 f_{n-1}(a,s,1)ds \\ x \geqslant a: & \int_0^1 f_{n-1}(x,s,2)ds \end{bmatrix}$$

$$f_n(a,x,0) = \begin{bmatrix} x < a: & \int_0^1 f_{n-1}(a,s,0)ds \\ x \geqslant a: & \max \begin{Bmatrix} \text{accept:} & \int_0^1 f_{n-1}(x,s,1)ds \\ \text{reject:} & \int_0^1 f_{n-1}(x,s,0)ds \end{Bmatrix} \end{bmatrix}$$

When $n = 0$, the target states are

$$(a,x,1) \text{ with } x < a$$

$$(a,x,0) \text{ with } x \geqslant a$$

and we may write

$$f_0(a,x,2) = 0$$

$$f_0(a,x,1) = 1, x < a$$
$$= 0, x \geqslant a$$

$$f_0(a,x,0) = 0, x < a$$
$$= 1, x \geqslant a$$

Thus

$$f_1(a,x,0) = \left[\begin{array}{ll} x < a: & \int_0^1 f_0(a,s,0)ds = 1 - a \\ x \geqslant a: & \max \left\{\begin{array}{l} \int_0^1 f_0(x,s,1)ds \\ \int_0^1 f_0(x,s,0)ds \end{array}\right\} \end{array}\right]$$

$$= \left[\begin{array}{ll} x < a: & 1 - a \\ x \geqslant a: & \max(x, 1 - x) \end{array}\right]$$

and so on.

In this second formulation it is as if we interview every candidate even when we have made a choice. The policy for this system is effectively the same as that for the first system in which we send home all the remaining candidates after the choice is made.

In the remainder of this section we shall use the first formulation, in which the remaining difficulties are all computational. Successive evaluation of the $f_n(.)$ gives

$$f_1(a,x) = \left[\begin{array}{l} x < a: \int_0^1 f_0(a,s)ds = 1 - a \\ x \geqslant a: \max \left\{\begin{array}{ll} \text{accept:} & x \\ \text{reject:} & \int_0^1 f_0(x,s)ds = 0 \int_0^x ds + 1 \int_x^1 ds = 1 - x \end{array}\right\} \\ \quad = \max(x, 1 - x) \end{array}\right]$$

Thus if the last candidate but one has the highest mark so far, we should choose her if her mark is more than 0.5 (or 50 on a 0-100 scale).

In computing $f_2(a,x)$ we need to split a and x into regions:

$$x < a: f_2(a,x) = \int_0^1 f_1(a,s)ds = \int_0^a f_1(a,s)ds + \int_a^1 f_1(a,s)ds$$

$$= \int_0^a (1-a)ds + \int_a^1 \max(s, 1-s)ds$$

and evaluating this expression separately for $a > \frac{1}{2}$ and $a < \frac{1}{2}$, we find

$$a > \frac{1}{2}: f_2(a,x) = \int_0^a (1-a)ds + \int_a^1 sds = (1-a)a + \frac{1}{2}(1-a^2) = \frac{1}{2} + a - \frac{3a^2}{2}$$

$$a < \frac{1}{2}: f_2(a,x) = \int_0^a (1-a)ds + \int_a^{\frac{1}{2}} (1-s)ds + \int_{\frac{1}{2}}^1 s\,ds$$

$$= (a-a^2) + \left(\frac{1}{2} - \frac{1}{8}\right) - \left(a - \frac{a^2}{2}\right) + \frac{1}{2} - \frac{1}{8} = \frac{3}{4} - \frac{a^2}{2}$$

$$x \geqslant a: f_2(a,x) = \max \begin{Bmatrix} x^2 \\ \\ \int_0^1 f_1(x,s)ds \end{Bmatrix}$$

$$x > \frac{1}{2}: f_2(a,x) = \max \begin{Bmatrix} x^2 \\ \\ \frac{1}{2} + x - \frac{3x^2}{2} \end{Bmatrix}$$

and the optimal decision is to choose this candidate if and only if she has the highest mark so far and

$$x^2 \geqslant \frac{1}{2} + x - \frac{3x^2}{2}$$

$$\text{i.e.} \quad 5x^2 - 2x - 1 \geqslant 0$$

$$\text{i.e.} \quad x \geqslant \frac{2+2\sqrt{6}}{10} \doteqdot 0.69$$

$$x < \frac{1}{2}: f_2(a,x) = \max \begin{Bmatrix} x^2 \\ \\ \frac{3}{4} - \frac{x^2}{2} \end{Bmatrix}$$

and the optimal decision is to reject this candidate, since

$$x^2 < \frac{3}{4} - \frac{x^2}{2} \text{ if } x < \frac{1}{2}$$

With four candidates in all, we now require only $f_3(0, x)$. We have

$$f_3(0,x) = \max \begin{Bmatrix} x^3 \\ \\ \int_0^1 f_2(x,s)ds \end{Bmatrix}$$

and for optimal decision-making we need to consider accepting this first candidate if her mark x is higher than $\frac{2+2\sqrt{6}}{10}$, when

$$\int_0^1 f_2(x,s)ds = \int_0^x \left(\frac{1}{2} + x - \frac{3x^2}{2}\right)ds + \int_x^1 s^2 ds$$

$$= \frac{1}{2}x + x^2 - \frac{3x^3}{2} + \frac{1}{3} - \frac{1}{3}x^3 = \frac{1}{3} + \frac{1}{2}x + x^2 - \frac{11}{6}x^3$$

Thus we should accept this first candidate if

$$x^3 \geqslant \frac{1}{3} + \frac{1}{2}x + x^2 - \frac{11}{6}x^3$$

i.e. $\quad x \geqslant 0.77$ (approximately).

It is interesting to compare the critical levels for accepting a candidate under the two criteria:

	Maximize expected mark	*Maximize probability of highest mark*
λ_0	0	0
λ_1	50	50
λ_2	63	69
λ_3	70	77

For interest, we compute $f_3(0,x)$ for values of x less than $\dfrac{2+2\sqrt{6}}{10} \doteqdot 0.69$.

$$\text{For } \frac{1}{2} < x < 0.69, \int_0^1 f_2(x,s)ds = \int_0^x \left(\frac{1}{2} + x - \frac{3x^2}{3}\right)ds + \int_x^{0.69} \left(\frac{1}{2} + s - \frac{3s^2}{2}\right)ds$$

$$+ \int_{0.69}^1 s^2 ds = \frac{1}{2}x + x^2 - \frac{3x^3}{2} + \left[\frac{1}{2}s + \frac{s^2}{2} - \frac{s^3}{2}\right]_x^{0.69} + \left[\frac{s^3}{3}\right]_{0.69}^1$$

$$= 0.643 + \frac{1}{2}x^2 - x^3$$

$$\text{For } 0 < x < \frac{1}{2}, \int_0^1 f_2(x,s) = \int_0^x \left(\frac{3}{4} - \frac{x^2}{2}\right)ds + \int_x^{\frac{1}{2}} \left(\frac{3}{4} - \frac{s^2}{2}\right)ds + \int_{\frac{1}{2}}^{0.69} \left(\frac{1}{2} + s - \frac{3s^2}{2}\right)ds$$

$$+ \int_{0.69}^1 s^2 ds = \frac{3}{4}x - \frac{x^3}{2} + \left[\frac{3}{4}s - \frac{s^3}{6}\right]_x^{\frac{1}{2}} + \left[\frac{1}{2}s + \frac{s^2}{2} - \frac{s^3}{2}\right]_{\frac{1}{2}}^{0.69}$$

$$+ \left[\frac{s^3}{3}\right]_{0.69}^1 = 0.685 - \frac{1}{3}x^3$$

Table 2.10 gives the optimal policy and state values.

	State region		$f_n(a,x)$	Optimal decision
$n=1$	$x < a$		$1 - a$	reject
	$x \geqslant a$	$x < \frac{1}{2}$	x	accept
		$x > \frac{1}{2}$	$1 - x$	reject
$n=2$	$x < a$	$a > \frac{1}{2}$	$\frac{1}{2} + a - \frac{3a^2}{2}$	reject
		$a < \frac{1}{2}$	$\frac{3}{4} - \frac{a^2}{2}$	reject
	$x \geqslant a$	$0.69 > x$	x^2	accept
		$\frac{1}{2} < x < 0.69$	$\frac{1}{2} + x - \frac{3x^2}{2}$	reject
		$x < \frac{1}{2}$	$\frac{3}{4} - \frac{x^2}{2}$	reject
$n=3$		$0.77 < x$	x^3	accept
		$0.69 < x < 0.77$	$\frac{1}{3} + \frac{1}{2}x + x^2 - \frac{11}{6}x^3$	reject
		$\frac{1}{2} < x < 0.69$	$0.645 + \frac{1}{2}x^2 - x^3$	reject
		$x < \frac{1}{2}$	$0.685 - \frac{1}{3}x^3$	reject

Table 2.10

Values of $f_n(a,x)$ for $x \geqslant a$ and $n = 0$ to 3 are shown in Figure 2.4. The figure confirms our intuitive ideas that if the first girl interviewed has a very high mark we accept her confidently, whereas if she has a low mark we reject her since we are fairly confident that a better candidate will appear among her successors; we are in fact more confident the lower the mark she has.

The reader may care to consider the game of Googol, in which a different number is written on each of N slips of paper which are turned upside down and shuffled.[11] The player picks them up in turn, looks at each number and when he thinks he has the highest number, he says so. If he is right, he wins; he cannot go back to a slip he has already seen. What is the policy which maximizes his probability of winning? (Hint: it may be convenient in this case to number the stages from the

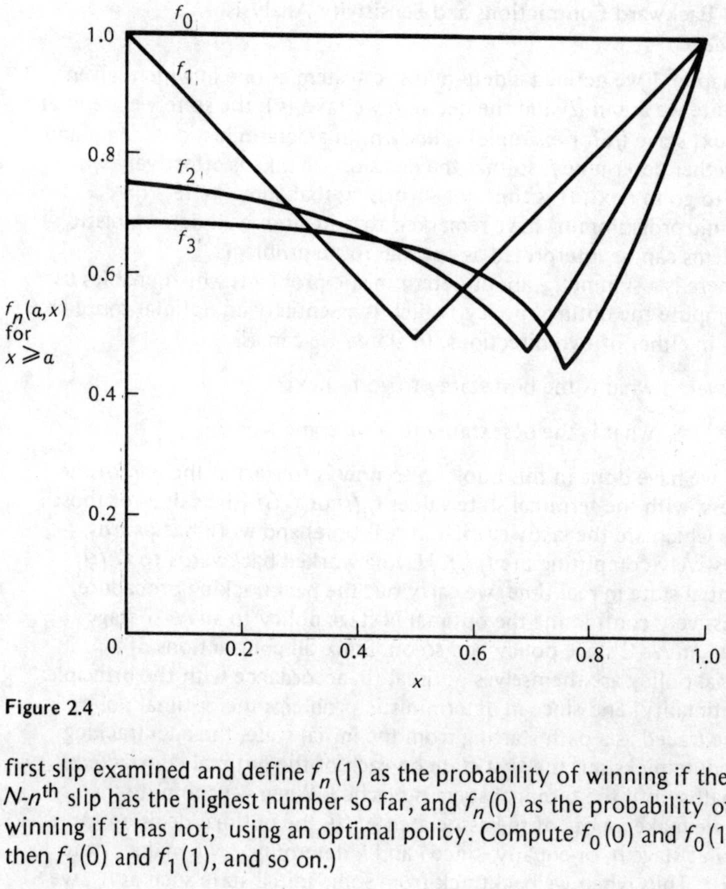

Figure 2.4

first slip examined and define $f_n(1)$ as the probability of winning if the N-n^{th} slip has the highest number so far, and $f_n(0)$ as the probability of winning if it has not, using an optimal policy. Compute $f_0(0)$ and $f_0(1)$, then $f_1(0)$ and $f_1(1)$, and so on.)

Conclusion

In both examples the problem characteristics – state, decisions and transitions – could be identified. However, the single-stage returns were missing and instead we had to define a terminal state which we desired to reach. In the first example the desired state was $(T\colon p_1, p_2, \ldots p_i \ldots p_s)$ with $p_i = 1$ for some i; in the second example the desired states were $(a,x,1)$ with $x < a$ and $(a,x,0)$ with $x \geqslant a$. In neither case was there any question of adding together returns or costs at each stage: the desired state was either reached or it was not reached.

An example of a final value system, not dealt with here, is trying to achieve a state as near as possible to some desired state. This kind of example, which is common in control engineering, is discussed by Aoki[2], some of whose work is summarized by Bellman and Dreyfus[7].

2.3 Backward Contractions and Sensitivity Analysis

Overview

In Chapter 1 we defined a deterministic system as one in which, given the state we are in (i) and the decision we take (k), the state we are in at the next stage (j, for example) is known. In a deterministic system i and k together determine j, so that the decision we take is effectively which state to go to next. It is thus not surprising that some writers on dynamic programming have remarked that in a sense all deterministic problems can be interpreted as optimal route problems.

There is a symmetry about deterministic problems which enables us to compute the optimal policy (which is essentially an optimal route or path) in either of two directions. In state i we can ask

either what is the best state j to go to next?

or what is the best state j to have come from?

What we have done in this book up to now is to start at the end of the process, with the terminal state values $f_0(i)$ or $f_1(i)$ (the values of those states which are the last we reach in real time) and work backwards, successively computing the $f_n(i)$. Having worked backwards to $f_N(i)$, the intial state in real time, we carry out the backtracking procedure, successively contracting the optimal N-stage policy to an $N-1$ stage policy, an $N-2$ stage policy and so on. Since all contractions of an optimal policy are themselves optimal (in accordance with the principle of optimality) and since in deterministic problems the optimal policy can be traced as a path starting from the initial state, the backtracking procedure picks out the first state on each of the optimal contracted sub-paths until the terminal stage is reached. When we compute the $f_n(i)$ we make a note of the associated $k_n^*(i)$, the optimal decision for state i at stage n, or equally, since i and k determine j, we make a note of $j_n^*(i)$. Thus when we backtrack from some initial state such as i_N, we trace the path comprising the successive states i_N, $j_N^*(i_N)$, $j_{N-1}^*(j_N^*(i_N))$, $j_{N-2}^*(j_{N-1}^*(j_N(i_N)))$, . . .

This entire process can be done in reverse. If we compute the best initial state (i.e. at the first stage) to have come from in order to be in any specific state at the second stage, we can then compute the best state to have come from at the second stage in order to be in any specific state at the third stage, and so on. The backtracking procedure would then pick out the terminal states on the optimal N-stage path, the optimal $N-1$ stage path, and so on until the initial stage is reached: in other words, it would contract the optimal policy backwards in time.

The forward contraction formulation is usually easier to express. Typically, we define $f_n(i)$ as the return associated with being in state i with n stages left, using an optimal policy; we ask what is the best decision k to take, if taking k will bring us to $j(=j^k(i))$ at the next stage? In the backward contraction formulation we typically define $F_n(i)$ as the return associated with being in some state i, n stages after the start of the process, having used an optimal policy; we ask what would have been the best decision k for us to have taken at the previous stage in order to have brought us to the state i $(=i^k(j))$ we are in now at stage n?

Here is one final way of expressing the difference (remembering that the symmetry only applies to deterministic problems):

in the forward contraction we choose which state we would do best to go to next

in the backward contraction we choose which state we would have done best to have been in previously.

Example: The electricity substation

A substation of size i can meet the demand for electricity in a certain area in each year n of a five-year period at a cost $C_n(i)$. A substation may be instantly replaced at the beginning of any year by a bigger substation of size j $(j > i)$ at a cost $R(j)$. With a discount factor* a, what sequence of substation sizes will minimise total discounted cost?

We first adopt the simply-expressed forward contraction formulation with which we are familiar. We define $f_n(i)$ as the total discounted cost associated with having a substation of size i, with n years left to the time horizon, using an optimal policy; optimal here means minimal total discounted cost. We note the characteristics of the problem:

State	*Decision*	*Single-stage costs*	*Transition*
Size i	keep i	$C_n(i)$	$i \to i$
	change to j	$C_n(j) + R(j)$	$i \to j$

and we may write

$$f_n(i) = \min \begin{bmatrix} \text{keep } i & : & C_n(i) + a\, f_{n-1}(i) \\ \text{change to } j: & & \min\limits_j \left(C_n(j) + R(j) + a\, f_{n-1}(j) \right) \end{bmatrix}$$

It is a simple matter to take care of the discount factor: the cost of proceeding optimally from the beginning of next year is simply discounted back to the beginning of this year.

The backward contraction formulation is a little more difficult to express. We define $F_n(i)$ as the total discounted cost associated with finishing up at the end of the nth year with a substation of size i, having

* If £100 now is thought to be equivalent to £100 + i in a year's time, then we may consider £100 in a year's time to be equivalent to £$\frac{100}{100+i}$ now. $\frac{100}{100+i} = a$ is called the discount factor; i is the interest rate.

used an optimal policy, optimal again meaning minimal total discounted cost. Notice that n in this formulation is an index counting the stages from the beginning of the 5-year period: in the forward contraction formulation n counts the stages from the end of the 5-year period. The characteristics of this formulation of the problem are

State	*Decision*	*Single-stage costs*	*Transition*
Size i	having kept the same size i	$K_n(i)$	$i \leftarrow i$
	having changed from size j to size i	$K_n(i) + R(i)$	$i \leftarrow j$

It is not a trivial task to identify the characteristics. If we change the substation size from j to i, we do so at a cost $R(i)$. We took this decision at the beginning of year n so we have this year incurred operating costs for a substation of size i. j is the size of the substation we had last year: the transition in real time has been from j to i. We may now write

$$F_n(i) = \min \begin{bmatrix} \text{having kept } i & : & a^{n-1}K_n(i) + F_{n-1}(i) \\ \text{having changed up from } j & : & \min\limits_j \left(a^{n-1}\left(K_n(i) + R(i)\right) + F_{n-1}(j) \right) \end{bmatrix}$$

It will be noted that the costs have been discounted to the beginning of the 5-year period. We could have discounted the costs similarly in the forward contraction formulation, but we instead adopted the neater method of discounting the value of optimal continuation from the transformed state one year at a time.

Table 2.11 gives illustrative numerical data, interpreted pictorially in Figure 2.5. The figure shows, for example, that in the last year only a substation of size 3 can meet the demand, so that the cost of operating a substation of size 1 or size 2 is infinite ($C_5(1) = K_1(1) = \infty$ and $C_5(2) = K_1(2) = \infty$).

	i	1	2	3	i	
	$R(i)$	4	6	7	$R(i)$	
Forward contraction formulation $C_n(i)$	n=5	3	4	6	n=1	Backward contraction formulation $K_n(i)$
	4	4	5	7	2	
	3	∞	6	9	3	
	2	∞	8	10	4	
	1	∞	∞	11	5	

a = 1 (i.e. no discounting)

Table 2.11

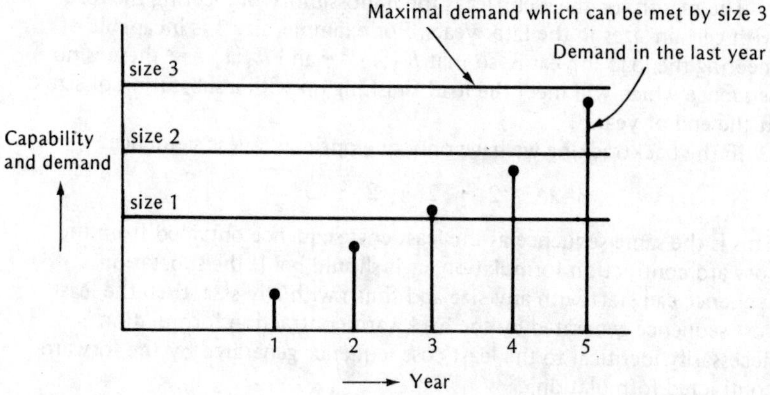

Figure 2.5

Using the forward contraction formulation, we may successively derive $f_1(i)$, $f_2(i)$ and so on to obtain Table 2.12.

i	$f_1(i)$	$j_1^*(i)$	$f_2(i)$	$j_2^*(i)$	$f_3(i)$	$j_3^*(i)$	$f_4(i)$	$j_4^*(i)$	$f_5(i)$	$j_5^*(i)$
1	18	3	28	3	37	3	41	1	44	1
2	18	3	26	2	32	2	37	2	41	2
3	11	3	21	3	30	3	37	3	43	3

Table 2.12

By backtracking, we find the following optimal 5-year sequences:

$$1 \to 1 \to 3 \to 3 \to 3$$
$$2 \to 2 \to 2 \to 2 \to 3$$
$$3 \to 3 \to 3 \to 3 \to 3$$

Using the backward contraction formulation, we may successively derive $F_1(i)$, $F_2(i)$ and so on, where the stages are numbered from the beginning of the process, and derive Table 2.13.

i	$F_1(i)$	$j_1^*(i)$	$F_2(i)$	$j_2^*(i)$	$F_3(i)$	$j_3^*(i)$	$F_4(i)$	$j_4^*(i)$	$F_5(i)$	$j_5^*(i)$
1	3	1	7	1	∞	·	∞	·	∞	·
2	4	2	9	2	15	2	23	2	∞	·
3	6	3	13	3	22	3	32	2 or 3	41	2

Table 2.13

The reason for the ∞ entries is the impossibility of meeting the load with certain sizes in the later years. For example, size 1 is incapable of meeting the load in year 3, so that $K_3(1) = \infty$ and $F_3(1) = \infty$: there is no sequence which will meet the load finishing up with a substation of size 1 at the end of year 3.

In the backtracking we have only one optimal 5-year sequence:

$$2 \rightarrow 2 \rightarrow 2 \rightarrow 2 \rightarrow 3$$

This is the same sequence as the least cost sequence obtained from the forward contraction formulation, as it should be. If the substation sequence can start with any size and finish with any size, then the least cost sequence generated by the backward contraction formulation is necessarily identical to the least cost sequence generated by the forward contracted formulation.

We can show how the two formulations differ by drawing a network of all possible substation sequences (Figure 2.6).

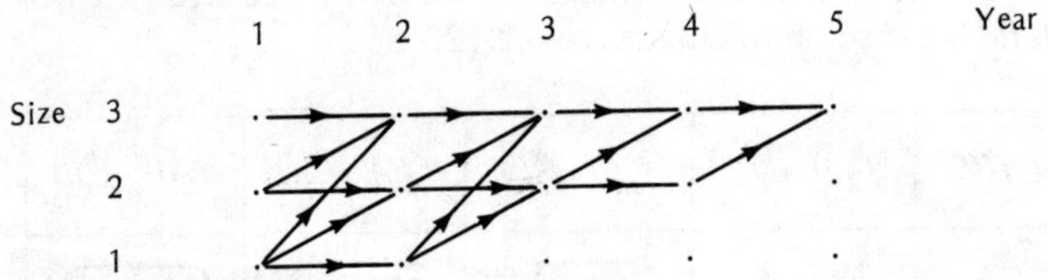

Figure 2.6

In the forward contraction formulation we find the optimal sequences from each permissible starting state (Figure 2.7).

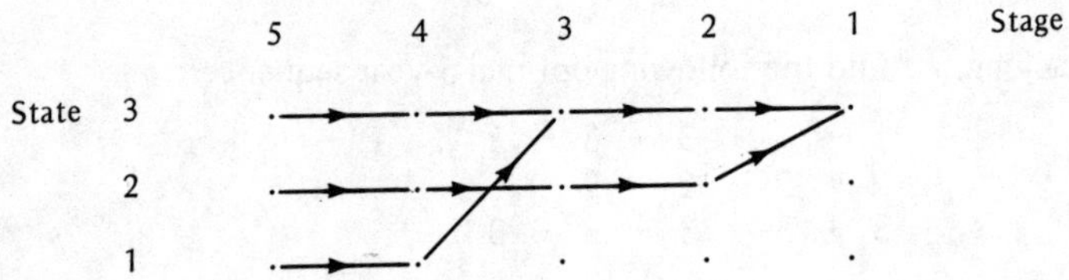

Figure 2.7

In the backward contraction formulation we find the optimal sequences ending in each permissible final state (Figure 2.8).

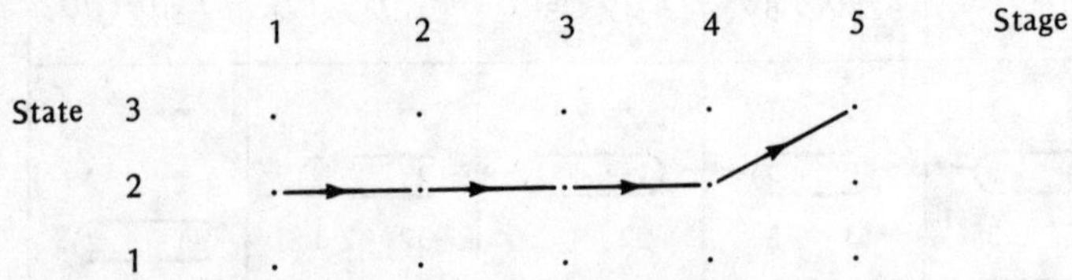

Figure 2.8

In the forward contraction formulation there are three permissible starting states (we can start with a substation of any size and even if one of them could not meet the load we could change up to a higher size immediately) and consequently there are three optimal sequences, each one starting from one of the permissible starting sizes. In the backward contraction formulation there is only one permissible final state and consequently only one optimal sequence, which terminates at the only permissible final size.

It must be noted that not all writers on dynamic programming use the terminology of this section which is based on White[21]. Many authors write of forward recursions and backward recursions, but it is not always immediately clear what they mean. Usually a backward recursion leads to a forward contracted policy, and vice versa. In White's terminology a forward contraction refers to a policy which is contracted forwards, though the calculations which led to that policy were carried out by working backwards from a time horizon (a terminal stage). White's usage of forward and backward, referring to the direction in which the policies are contracted, is to be preferred because it relates to the application of the principle of optimality.

One advantage of the backward contraction formulation is that the computations automatically provide a sensitivity analysis with respect to differing time horizons. The backward contraction formulation of the last example resulted in Table 2.14.

i	$F_1(i)$	$j_1^*(i)$	$F_2(i)$	$j_2^*(i)$	$F_3(i)$	$j_3^*(i)$	$F_4(i)$	$j_4^*(i)$	$F_5(i)$	$j_5^*(i)$
1	3	1	7	1	∞	.	∞	.	∞	.
2	4	2	9	2	15	2	23	2	∞	.
3	6	3	13	2	22	3	32	2 or 3	41	2

Table 2.14

If we backtrack from $F_1(1)$, $F_2(1)$, $F_3(2)$, $F_4(2)$, $F_5(3)$, since these are the costs of the minimum 1-year, 2-year, . . . 5-year size sequences when neither starting nor finishing size are specified, then we derive the five corresponding n-year sequences:

n	Optimal n-year sequence
5	2 → 2 → 2 → 2 → 3
4	2 → 2 → 2 → 2
3	2 → 2 → 2
2	1 → 1
1	1

with the corresponding cumulative costs:

n	Cumulative costs				
5	4	9	15	23	41
4	4	9	15	23	
3	4	9	15		
2	3	7			
1	3				

The reason that the sensitivity analysis is a by-product of the computations is that in order to compute $F_5(.)$ we need to know $F_4(.)$, in order to compute $F_4(.)$ we need to know $F_3(.)$, and so on.

Let us take a specific example. $F_3(2)$ is the cost of finishing up at the end of year 3 with a substation of size 2, having used an optimal policy, and $F_3(2)$ is smaller than both $F_3(1)$ and $F_3(3)$. Thus if we are free to choose any starting size, with a 3-year time horizon, we would built initially a substation of size 2 (and by backtracking from $F_3(2)$ we derive the optimal 3-year sequence $2 \rightarrow 2 \rightarrow 2$). However, the time horizon is actually 5 years and since $F_5(3)$ is smaller than both $F_5(1)$ and $F_5(2)$, we backtrack from $F_5(3)$ to find the optimal 5-year sequence $2 \rightarrow 2 \rightarrow 2 \rightarrow 2 \rightarrow 3$. Over the first three years this sequence is identical to the optimal 3-year sequence, so that if the time horizon in the event turns out to be 3 years and not 5 years, we shall lose nothing since we shall have carried out the optimal 3-year policy anyway.

To put this in a practical context, suppose it is required to install generating equipment to supply electricity to a remote island on which a battalion of troops is to be stationed, probably for 5 years, possibly less, but certainly not more. With the given data, if the troops leave the island after 3 years but we have planned for them to stay 5, we have lost nothing. Suppose however they stay for only 2 years. The optimal 2-year sequence is $1 \rightarrow 1$, costing 7, while the truncated 2-year sequence derived from the optimal 5-year sequence is $2 \rightarrow 2$, costing 9. In this case, planning for a 5-year stay when the stay is only 2 years would result in an excess of a little over 28% $(= \frac{2}{7})$.

Conclusion

In general, if we let π_n define an optimal n-year policy and $C(\pi_n, m)$ define the cost of operating this policy over m years $(m < n)$, then in carrying out a sensitivity analysis with respect to time horizon, we compare

$$C(\pi_m, m) \text{ with } C(\pi_n, m)$$

The question we want to answer is how much would we lose if the time horizon were only m years and not n years? We want to find out how much worse off we would be operating a policy which is optimal for a time horizon n if the actual time horizon turns out to be m. In some texts sensitivity analysis is interpreted as the comparison of $C(\pi_m,m)$ with $C(\pi_n,n)$, but such a comparison is not very revealing as it only shows the difference in cost between the optimal m-year policy and the optimal n-year policy, which has no practical significance. A true sensitivity analysis should show how serious the effects might be of operating a chosen policy if circumstances were to change or if parameters have been inaccurately estimated. A policy which differs little in cost from the costs of the policies which are optimal in changed circumstances is sometimes called robust. The 5-year sequence is quite robust in this sense, in that the truncated policies derived from it will be optimal unless the actual time horizon is as short as 2 years. The robustness of a policy is an important factor in considering its adoption: when data are uncertain it may be preferable to be cautious and adopt a policy which will give lower returns but will not be costly even if the parameters are wrong, rather than a policy which will give high returns only if the parameters are right and will otherwise lose money.

3 Other Computational Methods

3.1 Approximation in Policy Space

Overview

In all the preceding examples the computational technique has been to successively evaluate the $f_n(.)$, a technique sometimes known as value iteration. When the $f_n(.)$ converge to a limiting value $f(.)$, as in the optimal route problem, the technique is properly called approximation in function space. To recapitulate, what we did was to successively evaluate

$$f_n(i) = \min_j \left[c(i,j) + f_{n-1}(j) \right]$$

and we showed that the values of $f_n(i)$ did not decrease after $n = 5$.

In cases where it is required to solve functional equations such as $f(i) = \min_{j \neq i} [c(i,j) + f(j)]$, it is possible to use an alternative technique known as approximation in policy space.

Example: optimal route

In the optimal route problem, this would involve firstly guessing the best town to go to next (the optimal $j^*(i)$), making sure that the policy contains no loops, and then solving the functional equations, one for each town. Suppose we guess that $j^*(1) = 2$, $j^*(2) = 3$, $j^*(3) = 4$ and so on; the set of functional equations is

$$\begin{aligned} f(1) &= c(1,2) + f(2) \\ f(2) &= c(2,3) + f(3) \\ f(3) &= c(3,4) + f(4) \\ f(4) &= c(4,5) + f(5) \\ f(5) &= c(5,6) + f(6) \\ f(6) &= c(6,6) + f(6) \end{aligned}$$

For a real-life interpretation, we must have $f(6) = 0$, and we can then solve these equations to give

$$\begin{aligned} f(1) &= 57 \\ f(2) &= 32 \\ f(3) &= 27 \\ f(4) &= 11 \\ f(5) &= 3 \\ f(6) &= 0 \end{aligned}$$

We then use these values of *f(i)* in the right hand sides of the functional equations (sometimes known as the test quantity in this context) to determine an improved policy. Thus, for town 1,

$$\min \begin{bmatrix} j{=}2: & c(1,2) + f(2) \\ j{=}3: & c(1,3) + f(3) \\ j{=}4: & c(1,4) + f(4) \\ j{=}5: & c(1,5) + f(5) \\ j{=}6: & c(1,6) + f(6) \end{bmatrix}$$

$$= \min \begin{bmatrix} 25 + 32 \\ 15 + 27 \\ \infty + 11 \\ 34 + \;\;3 \\ \infty + \;\;0 \end{bmatrix} \leftarrow$$

$$= 37, \text{ and } j^*(1) = 5$$

In the same way, using the same values of *f(i)*, we can derive new decisions for the other states:

$$j^*(2) = 4$$
$$j^*(3) = 6$$
$$j^*(4) = 5$$
$$j^*(5) = 6$$
$$j^*(6) = 6$$

and use these decisions in turn to derive a new set of functional equations:

$$f(1) = c(1,5) + f(5)$$
$$f(2) = c(2,4) + f(4)$$
$$f(3) = c(3,6) + f(6)$$
$$f(4) = c(4,5) + f(5)$$
$$f(5) = c(5,6) + f(6)$$
$$f(6) = 0$$

whose solution is

$$f(1) = 37$$
$$f(2) = 15$$
$$f(3) = 22$$
$$f(4) = 11$$
$$f(5) = 3$$
$$f(6) = 0$$

Again, we use these values of *f(i)* in the functional equations to determine an improved policy (if there is one). Thus for town 1,

$$\min \begin{bmatrix} j=2: & c(1,2) + f(2) \\ j=3: & c(1,3) + f(3) \\ j=4: & c(1,4) + f(4) \\ j=5: & c(1,5) + f(5) \\ j=6: & c(1,6) + f(6) \end{bmatrix}$$

$$= \min \begin{bmatrix} 25 + 15 \\ 15 + 22 \\ \infty + 11 \\ 34 + 3 \\ \infty + 0 \end{bmatrix} \begin{matrix} \\ \leftarrow \\ \\ \leftarrow \\ \\ \end{matrix}$$

$$= 37, \text{ and } j^*(1) = 3 \text{ or } 5$$

In the same way, we can derive improved decisions for the other states to give the following:

$$\begin{aligned} j^*(2) &= 4 \\ j^*(3) &= 2 \\ j^*(4) &= 5 \\ j^*(5) &= 6 \\ j^*(6) &= 6 \end{aligned}$$

and if $j^*(1)$ is taken as 3, the process will converge at the next iteration, giving the same optimal policy as was found earlier, in the optimal route problem in Section 2.1 (p. 17).

The new functional equations are

$$\begin{aligned} f(1) &= c(1,3) + f(3) \\ f(2) &= c(2,4) + f(4) \\ f(3) &= c(3,2) + f(2) \\ f(4) &= c(4,5) + f(5) \\ f(5) &= c(5,6) + f(6) \\ f(6) &= 0 \end{aligned}$$

whose solutions are

$$\begin{aligned} f(1) &= 35 \\ f(2) &= 15 \\ f(3) &= 20 \\ f(4) &= 11 \\ f(5) &= 3 \\ f(6) &= 0 \end{aligned}$$

These values are identical to those found in Section 2.1. Had $j^*(1)$ been taken as 5 instead of 3 in this iteration, a further iteration would have been necessary before convergence was reached.

That convergence has occurred may be verified by trying to find an improved policy. Thus for town 1,

$$\min \begin{bmatrix} j{=}2\colon & c(1,2) + f(2) \\ j{=}3\colon & c(1,3) + f(3) \\ j{=}4\colon & c(1,4) + f(4) \\ j{=}5\colon & c(1,5) + f(5) \\ j{=}6\colon & c(1,6) + f(6) \end{bmatrix}$$

$$= \min \begin{bmatrix} 25 + 15 \\ 15 + 20 \\ \infty + 11 \\ 34 + 3 \\ \infty + 0 \end{bmatrix} \longleftarrow$$

$$= 35 \text{ and } j^*(1) = 3 \text{ as before.}$$

If similar calculations are carried out, no improved decision will be found for any of the other towns.

Conclusion

The two methods of computation considered so far (in this section and Section 2.1) in relation to the optimal route problem are shown in Figure 3.1 in the form of flow charts.

When approximating in policy space we may expect the number of iterations to be small if the initial policy $\left\{ j_1^*(i) \right\}$ is close to the optimal, so that the computational burden will be less than that of approximating in function space. However, when the computational burden is heavy it is usually not because of the time taken by the iterations, but because of the computer storage required for the state values. In such a case approximating in policy space, which involves the solution of as many equations as there are states at each iteration, may be impracticable.

Both the techniques can strictly be used only for processes which have an infinite number of stages, but when there is a finite number of stages, then the computations carried out in the method of successively computing the $f_n(.)$, stepping back one stage at a time from the time horizon, are identical to those which would be carried out in an infinite-stage process using approximation in function space. This is perhaps a reason for the intuitive appeal of the latter method.

The most notable development of the technique of approximation in policy space, relating particularly to stochastic processes, has been achieved by R. A. Howard[10] whose short book on this topic is recommended.

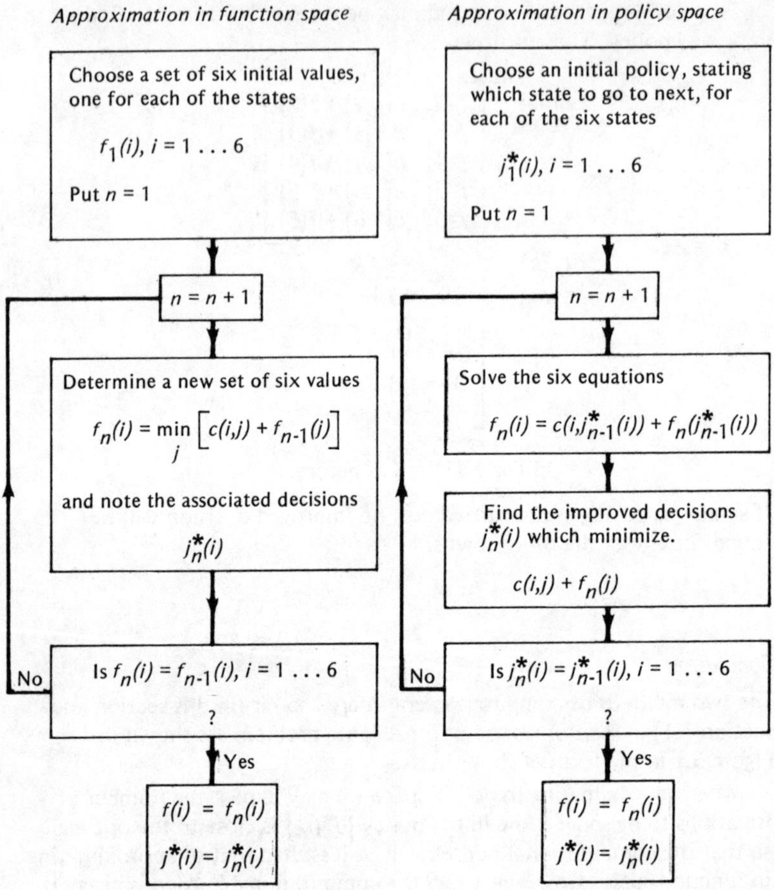

Figure 3.1

3.2 Computation for Directed States

Overview

In some problems in dynamic programming, the states may be ordered in some well-defined, regular fashion and it may be possible to compute the optimal policy and the associated values for each possible initial state without making use of the notion of stages.

Examples

Optimal route We first consider the optimal route problem of Section 2.1 (p. 10), with the additional constraint that we can go from town i to town j only if j is a number at least as large as i. In other words, we can go directly from town 1 to town 5, for instance, but not from town 5 to town 1. The permissible transitions may be marked on the map as in Figure 3.2; the only difference from Figure 2.1 on page 10 is the addition of these permissible transitions, marked by arrows.

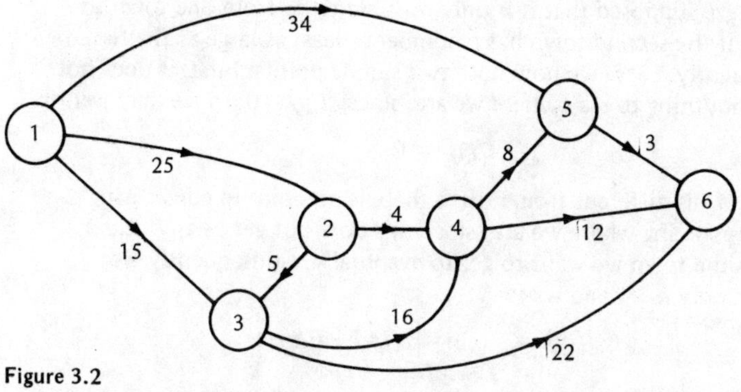

Figure 3.2

The table of costs now effectively comprises only the top right half of the original table, and may be written as Table 3.1.

		to j					
		1	2	3	4	5	6
from i	1	0	25	15	∞	34	∞
	2		0	5	4	∞	∞
	3			0	16	∞	22
	4				0	8	12
	5					0	3
	6						0

Table 3.1

All the other $c(i,j)$ entries are now equal to ∞, and are not shown.

Suppose that we wish to find the optimal route not just from any town i to town 6 but from any town i to any other town j. We could define $f(i,j)$ as the cost of going from town i to town j, using an optimal policy where optimal means least cost, as before. The decision we have to take if we are in town i is which town to go to next; we may call this town k. For this kind of deterministic problem the transition rule is easy: if we decide to go to town k next, town k is the next town we shall be in and from town k onwards we shall want to proceed to town j

in an optimal manner. Since the cost of doing so is $f(k,j)$, we may write

$$f(i,j) = \min_{k \neq i} \left[c(i,k) + f(k,j) \right]$$

We have supposed that it is only possible to go from one town to another if the second town has a number at least as large as the first. Consequently $k \geqslant i$. We now note two simple points. First, it does not cost us anything to stay where we are, since $c(i,i) = 0$, so we may write

$$f(i,i) = 0$$

Second, if j is different from i, then there is no point in considering $k = i$ (i.e. staying where we are) since this does not get us any nearer j which is the town we want to get to eventually. Consequently we consider only $k > i$ and write

$$f(i,j) = \min_{j \geqslant k > i} \left[c(i,k) + f(k,j) \right]$$

We can now compute all the $f(i,j)$ directly. For example, we know $f(1,1)$, $f(2,2)$ . . . $f(6,6)$: they are all zero. $f(1,2)$, $f(2,3)$ . . . $f(5,6)$ can now be computed: they are equal to $c(1,2)$, $c(2,3)$ . . . $c(5,6)$. After that we can compute $f(1,3)$, $f(2,4)$, $f(3,5)$ and $f(4,6)$, and following them $f(1,4)$, $f(2,5)$ and $f(3,6)$, then $f(1,5)$ and $f(2,6)$ and finally $f(1,6)$. For example we note that

$$f(1,3) = \min \begin{bmatrix} k = 2\text{:} \;\; c(1,2) + f(2,3) \\ \\ k = 3\text{:} \;\; c(1,3) + f(3,3) \end{bmatrix}$$

and that in this sequence of computation $f(2,3)$ and $f(3,3)$ will have already been computed. Again, we note that

$$f(1,4) = \min \begin{bmatrix} k = 2\text{:} \;\; c(1,2) + f(2,4) \\ k = 3\text{:} \;\; c(1,3) + f(3,4) \\ k = 4\text{:} \;\; c(1,4) + f(4,4) \end{bmatrix}$$

and that in this sequence of computation $f(2,4)$, $f(3,4)$, and $f(4,4)$ will have already been computed.

This is not the only possible sequence for computing the $f(i,j)$. An alternative is to compute $f(6,6)$; then $f(5,5)$ and $f(5,6)$; then $f(4,4)$, $f(4,5)$ and $f(4,6)$; then $f(3,3)$, $f(3,4)$, $f(3,5)$, $f(3,6)$; then $f(2,2)$ and so on, finishing with $f(1,6)$.

It is a worthwhile numerical exercise to confirm the values and the associated decisions of Tables 3.2 and 3.3.

$\{f(i,j)\}$

i \ j	1	2	3	4	5	6
1	0	25	15	29	34	37
2		0	5	4	12	15
3			0	16	24	22
4				0	8	11
5					0	3
6						0

Table 3.2

$\{k^*(i,j)\}$

i \ j	1	2	3	4	5	6
1	1	2	3	2	5	3 or 5
2		2	3	4	4	4
3			3	4	4	6
4				4	5	5
5					5	6
6						6

Table 3.3

The first steps are straightforward. $f(6,6) = 0$ and the associated decision is $k^*(6,6) = 6$: if we are in town 6 and we want to go to town 6, the next town to go to is town 6 and it costs us nothing to get there. Similarly $f(5,5) = 0$ and $k^*(5,5) = 5$.

$$\begin{aligned} f(5,6) &= c(5,6) + f(6,6) \\ &= 3 + 0 \\ &= 3 \\ \text{and } k^*(5,6) &= 6 \end{aligned}$$

It is easy to show that $f(4,4) = 0$, $f(4,5) = 8$ and to write down the associated decisions. For $f(4,6)$, we write

$$f(4,6) = \min \begin{bmatrix} k=5: & c(4,5) + f(5,6) = 8 + 3 = 11 \leftarrow \\ k=6: & c(4,6) + f(6,6) = 12 + 0 = 12 \end{bmatrix}$$

$= 11$, and we note that $k^*(4,6) = 5$.

In the same way, the whole table of $f(i,j)$ can be completed, the last calculation being

$$f(1,6) = \min \begin{bmatrix} k=2: & c(1,2) + f(2,6) = 25 + 15 = 40 \\ k=3: & c(1,3) + f(3,6) = 15 + 22 = 37 \leftarrow \\ k=4: & c(1,4) + f(4,6) = \infty + 11 = \infty \\ k=5: & c(1,5) + f(5,6) = 34 + 3 = 37 \leftarrow \\ k=6: & c(1,6) + f(6,6) = \infty + 0 = \infty \end{bmatrix}$$

$= 37$,

giving $k^*(1,6) = 3$ or 5

Obviously, some of the values for $f(i,6)$ are greater than the corresponding values for $f(i)$ obtained earlier. For example, it costs 37 to go from town 1 to town 6 if transitions are only allowed to higher numbered towns, but it costs 35 without this restriction. The optimal route can be read from the $k^*(i,j)$ table; for example, the optimal routes from town 1 to town 6 in the restricted problem are

$1 \rightarrow 3 \rightarrow 6$ (costing $15 + 22 = 37$)

and $1 \rightarrow 5 \rightarrow 6$ (costing $34 + 3 = 37$)

since for the first alternative $k^*(1,6) = 3$, $k^*(3,6) = 6$, and for the second alternative $k^*(1,6) = 5$, $k^*(5,6) = 6$.

It is worth noting that the method of successive evaluation may still be used for this problem. We may define $f_n(i,j)$ as the cost of going from town i to town j $(j \geqslant i)$ under an optimal policy, in at most n steps, where optimal means least cost, and compute $\{f_1(i,j)\}$, $\{f_2(i,j)\}$, $\{f_3(i,j)\}$ and so on, and then find the optimal routes by backtracking just as before in Section 2.1. However, the computational burden will be rather heavier.

The table for $\{f_1(i,j)\}$ is identical to the $\{c(i,j)\}$ table, with $k^*(i,j) = j$. The tables of $\{f_2(i,j)\}$ and $\{k_2^*(i,j)\}$ (Tables 3.4 and 3.5) are shown below.

$\{f_2(i,j)\}$

i \ j	1	2	3	4	5	6
1	0	25	15	29	34	37
2		0	5	4	12	15
3			0	16	24	22
4				0	8	11
5					0	3
6						0

Table 3.4

$\{k_2^*(i,j)\}$

i \ j	1	2	3	4	5	6
1	1	2	3	2	5	3 or 5
2		2	3	4	4	4
3			3	4	4	6
4				4	5	5
5					5	6
6						6

Table 3.5

The table for $\{f_3(i,j)\}$ (and for $\{f_4(i,j)\}$ and $\{f_5(i,j)\}$) is identical to the table for $\{f(i,j)\}$ already found using the direct method.

Finally, it is interesting to put the problem into a practical context taken from White[23]. Brass strip of a certain gauge i enters a rolling mill, to be reduced to strip of another gauge j. The operation can sometimes be done directly at a cost $c(i,j)$, but it may be better to carry out the reduction via one or more intermediate gauges k (see Figure 3.3). What is the optimal reduction sequence for each combination of gauges i-j?

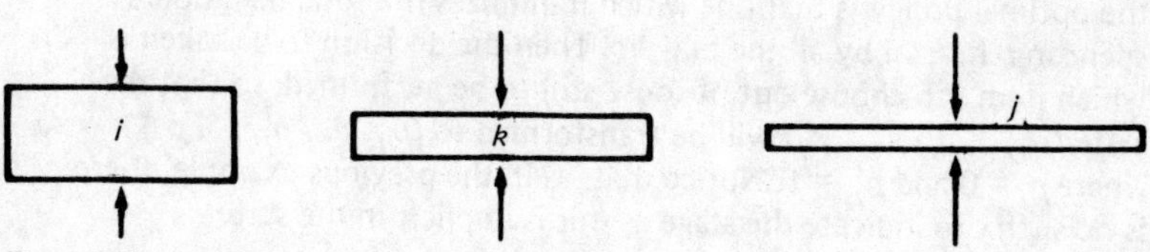

Figure 3.3

Once it is noted that a larger gauge corresponds to a smaller width, the correspondence with the restricted optimal route problem is exact. The gauges correspond to the towns and the single-stage rolling costs correspond to the single-step costs of travelling between two towns. The infinite cost associated with some of the single-stage rolling reductions can be interpreted as the non-availability of rolling machinery capable of carrying out those particular reductions. In the example discussed in White's thesis there are 22 gauges instead of 6 and the $c(i,j)$ are slightly more complicated functions, but the difference between the 6-state problem and the 22-state problem is primarily one of size, not of complexity. It is interesting that such an artificial exercise as the restricted optimal route problem has an exact counterpart in an actual industrial problem.

The orchestra rehearsal Not every player in an orchestra is required for every piece that is to be practised at a rehearsal. If every player arrives just in time for the first piece for which he is required and leaves immediately after the last piece for which he is required, in what order should the pieces be played so as to minimise the total time (in man-hours) spent by the orchestra in rehearsal?

This problem is simple to state but difficult to formulate. Let there be r pieces which have to be rehearsed and let the ith piece last a time t_i.

Define $\theta(i,j) = 1$ if piece i requires player j.
$= 0$ otherwise.

It is easy enough to imagine the orchestra having played a number of pieces and then deciding which piece to play next. It seems reasonable to think of the description of the system as a list of those pieces which have already been played, the decision as which piece to play next and the transformed state as the state of the system after this next piece has been played.

Let the state be described by a list of ones and zeros $(p_1, p_2, \ldots p_r)$

where $p_i = 1$ if the ith piece has already been played
$= 0$ otherwise

and let $f(p_1, p_2, \ldots p_r)$ be the total man-hours required to rehearse the remaining items (those for which $p_i = 0$) using an optimal policy, where the optimal policy is that one which minimizes the total man-hours spent in rehearsal by all the players. Then the decision to be taken is which item i to choose out of those still to be performed, so that the state $(p_1, \ldots p_i, \ldots p_r)$ will be transformed to $(p_1, \ldots p_i', \ldots p_r)$ where $p_i = 0$ and $p_i' = 1$. Notice that, as in the previous example, there is no suffix to indicate the stage as this is implicit in the state description.

The difficulty in this problem is in working out the single-stage costs. If we decide to play piece *i* next, then we need to add to the total time required for the rest of the rehearsal t_i for each player required for this piece. However, this is not all: those players not required for this piece, who have already played in a previous piece and still have at least one piece left to play, must be taken into account as well. There is more than one way of expressing this; the notation used in the following treatment is only one alternative.

$$\text{Define } l_j = 1 \text{ if } \sum_{\substack{i \text{ such that} \\ p_i = 1}} \theta(i,j) > 0 \text{ and } \sum_{\substack{i \text{ such that} \\ p_i = 0}} \theta(i,j) > 0$$

$$= 0 \text{ otherwise}$$

In other words, $l_j = 1$ if player *j* has already played and still has at least one other piece to play. We need to avoid counting twice players who have already played, have still to play and are needed for piece *i*. To avoid such double counting we introduce the symbol $\oplus$ and define

$$a \oplus b = 0 \text{ if } a = b = 0$$

$$= 1$$ otherwise (i.e. if either or both of *a* and *b* is not equal to zero)

We may now write

$$f(p_1, \ldots p_r) = \min_{\substack{i \text{ such that} \\ p_i = 0}} \left[t_i \left(\sum_j \left(\theta(i,j) \oplus l_j \right) \right) + f(p_1, \ldots p_i', \ldots p_r) \right]$$

In effect, in computing the single-stage costs we add on t_i (the duration of the ith piece) for each player who is

either performing the ith piece $[\theta(i,j) = 1]$
or who has already performed and has still to perform $[l_j = 1]$
or both.

What we need in the end is of course $f(0 \ldots 0)$.

The computation is, like most computations in dynamic programming, tedious but straightforward. The states are ordered, so that starting with $f(1 \ldots . 1)$, we can compute $f(111 \ldots . 10)$, $f(111 \ldots . 101)$, $f(11 \ldots . 011) \ldots \ldots$ and finally $f(0 \ldots . 0)$.

As an illustration, consider the case of a rehearsal in which 4 pieces are to be rehearsed, altogether requiring 5 players (see Table 3.6).

$\{\theta(i,j)\}$

	Player j 1	2	3	4	5	Duration t_i
Piece i 1	1	1	1		1	2
2		1		1		1
3		1	1	1	1	3
4		1			1	1

Table 3.6

If the pieces are rehearsed in the order 1–2–3–4, then the total time spent will be 26 man-hours, made up as follows:

Player	*Attendance time*
1	2
2	7
3	6
4	4
5	7
	26

Players 3 and 5 each lose one hour while piece 2 is played.

The computations carried out to determine the optimal sequence are shown in Table 3.7. After the states have been listed, the values of l_j for each state can be computed. For example, in state 0110 $l_2 = l_3 = l_5 = 1$ since players 2, 3 and 5 have already played (player 2 in piece 2; players 2, 3 and 5 in piece 3) and still have at least one piece to play (players 2 and 5 are needed for both piece 1 and piece 4; player 3 is needed for piece 1). $l_1 = 0$ since player 1 has not yet played; $l_4 = 0$ since player 4 has played both his pieces and is no longer required. The alternatives for each state are simply a list of possible pieces to play next. The two figures in the test quantity represent respectively the single-stage costs and the costs of the transformed state. Thus in state 0110, if piece 1 is played next, the single-stage cost is 8 (players 1, 2, 3 and 5 rehearsing for 2 hours) and $f(1110)$ is 2. Again in state 0110, if piece 4 is played next the single-stage cost is 3 (players 2 and 5 rehearsing for 1 hour and player 3 hanging about for the same time) and $f(0111)$ is 8. The smaller test quantity has the value 10 and the associated decision is to play piece 1 next.

State	l_1 l_2 l_3 l_4 l_5	Alternative	Test quantity	Decision
1 1 1 1	0 0 0 0 0		0	–
1 1 1 0	0 1 0 0 1	4	2 + 0 = 2	4
1 1 0 1	0 1 1 1 1	3	12 + 0 = 12	3
1 0 1 1	0 1 0 1 0	2	2 + 0 = 2	2
0 1 1 1	0 1 1 0 1	1	8 + 0 = 8	1
1 1 0 0	0 1 1 1 1	3 4	12 + 2 = 14 ← 4 + 12 = 16	3
1 0 1 0	0 1 0 1 1	2 4	3 + 2 = 5 ← 3 + 2 = 5 ←	2 or 4
1 0 0 1	0 1 1 0 1	2 3	4 + 12 = 16 12 + 2 = 14 ←	3
0 1 1 0	0 1 1 0 1	1 4	8 + 2 = 10 ← 3 + 8 = 11	1
0 1 0 1	0 1 0 1 1	1 3	10 + 12 = 22 12 + 8 = 20 ←	3
0 0 1 1	0 1 1 1 1	1 2	10 + 2 = 12 ← 4 + 8 = 12 ←	1 or 2
1 0 0 0	0 1 1 0 1	2 3 4	4 + 14 = 18 12 + 5 = 17 ← 3 + 14 = 17 ←	3 or 4
0 1 0 0	0 1 0 1 0	1 3 4	10 + 14 = 24 12 + 10 = 22 ← 3 + 20 = 23	3
0 0 1 0	0 1 1 1 1	1 2 4	10 + 5 = 15 4 + 10 = 14 ← 4 + 12 = 16	2
0 0 0 1	0 1 0 0 1	1 2 3	8 + 14 = 22 ← 3 + 20 = 23 12 + 12 = 24	1
0 0 0 0	0 0 0 0 0	1 2 3 4	8 + 17 = 25 2 + 22 = 24 ← 12 + 14 = 26 2 + 22 = 24 ←	2 or 4

Table 3.7

It will be seen that there are two alternative optimal rehearsal programs, 2–3–1–4 and 4–1–3–2, each having a total rehearsal time of 24 man-hours. The schedules for the two sequences are shown in Tables 3.8 and 3.9.

Piece \ Player	1	2	3	4	5
2		1		1	
3		1	1	1	1
1	1	1	1		1
4		1			1

Table 3.8

Piece \ Player	1	2	3	4	5
4		1			1
1	1	1	1		1
3		1	1	1	1
2		1		1	

Table 3.9

It will be noticed that these sequences are reversals of each other and that no player has to hang about at all.

If n pieces are to be rehearsed, then in this formulation the number of states is 2^n and this number can be very large for relatively small values of n. Nevertheless, in comparison with the explicit enumeration of all possible sequences the dynamic programming computation is very efficient. If there are n pieces to be rehearsed, then there are $n!$ possible sequences (n choices for the first piece, n-1 for the second, and so on). A comparison of values of 2^n and $n!$ (as in Table 3.10) for a few values of n is instructive.

n	2^n	$n!$
1	2	1
2	4	2
3	8	6
4	16	24
5	32	120
6	64	720
7	128	5040
8	256	40320
9	512	362880
10	1024	3628800

Table 3.10

The numerical difference between the corresponding values of 2^n and $n!$ overstates the difference in the computational burden, since there is on average more work in computing the test quantities for each of the 2^n states than there is computing the man hours involved in each of the $n!$ program sequences, but the difference in the computational burden is marked even for low values of n.

Puzzles The third example is frequently found in puzzles: more practical examples may be concerned with sorting and/or searching, when it is required to locate one or more items in a set in the minimal number of operations. The objective is to transform a system from one state to another state in the minimal number of transitions, such that reaching the final state can be guaranteed. Examples of such an objective occur in the following problems:

(a) A set of otherwise indistinguishable snooker balls contain one which is heavier than the others. Find the minimal number of weighings required to determine the heavier ball.

(b) A number of cannibals and a number of missionaries have one boat of limited capacity in which to cross a river. At all times (in the boat and on either river bank) the missionaries must at least equal the cannibals. Find the minimal number of trips required to transport all the missionaries and all the cannibals across the river.

(c) Two vessels have 5 pint and 7 pint capacities respectively. Find the minimal number of operations needed to leave 3 pints of water in the 5-pint vessel and the 7-pint vessel empty.

Such puzzles are easy to formulate in terms of dynamic programming, but the resulting computation is usually tedious. Taking example (c) as a case in point, we note that the state is described by the amount of water in each vessel (for example X and Y). The possible decisions are as follows:

k = 1 fill the 5-pint vessel from a tap
2 pour as much as possible from the 7-pint vessel into the 5-pint vessel
3 empty the 5-pint vessel
4 fill the 7-pint vessel from a tap
5 pour as much as possible from the 5-pint vessel into the 7-pint vessel
6 empty the 7-pint vessel

The single-stage costs are simply those of carrying out another operation; the transformed states resulting from the six transitions are shown in Table 3.11.

Decision k	Transformed state X'_k	Y'_k
1	5	Y
2	min $(5, X+Y)$	max $(0, X+Y-5)$
3	0	Y
4	X	7
5	max $(0, X+Y-7)$	min $(7, X+Y)$
6	X	0

Table 3.11

Thus if we define $f(X, Y)$ as the number of steps required to leave 3 pints of water in the first vessel, now having X pints in the first and Y in the second, using an optimal policy we may write

$$f(X, Y) = \min_k \left[1 + f(X'_k, Y'_k)\right]$$

$$= 1 + \min_k \left[f(X'_k, Y'_k)\right]$$

$$\text{with } f(3,0) = 0$$

We require eventually $f(0,0)$.

Clearly $f(3, Y) = 1$ for all $Y (k^* = 6)$ and in particular $f(3,7) = 1$, so that $f(5,5) = 2$, and so on.

Since our aim in this section is to illustrate the formulation rather than the computation, we remark only that by backtracking on completio of the computation, the optimal sequence will be found to be

$$(0,0) \rightarrow (5,0) \rightarrow (0,5) \rightarrow (5,5) \rightarrow (3,7) \rightarrow (3,0)$$

with the associated sequence of decisions

$$1 \rightarrow 5 \rightarrow 1 \rightarrow 5 \rightarrow 6$$

Conclusion

The method of computation for directed states is not a special case of value iteration; in fact, the reverse is the case. If the stage is considered as part of the state description, so that for computational purposes $f_n(.)$ is treated as $f(n,.)$, then the states $(n,.)$ are themselves ordered and in successively evaluating the $f_n(.)$ we effectively evaluate $f(n,.)$.

4 Computational Problems

4.1 Dimensionality

Overview

In all the preceding chapters the computation involved in the successive evaluation of the $f_n(.)$ has been done by hand. In each case the right-hand side of the functional equation was evaluated for each alternative in each state at every stage. If we worked in FORTRAN we might have three nested DO loops: one for the alternatives, one for the states and one for the stages. The reason we did not write computer programs for the computations is that it would not have been worthwhile; the computational burden was small. In the optimal route problem there were 5 alternatives, 5 states and 4 stages; in the problem of selling the car there were 2 alternatives, 4 states and 20 stages: in neither of them were there many calculations to do.

Suppose, however, that in some problem we work out the successive $f_n(.)$ using a computer. A typical functional equation of level 0 is

$$f_n(i) = \max_k \left[q_i^k + f_{n-1}(j) \right]$$

where i is the current state
j is the transformed state
n and n-1 are indices referring to the stage
k is the decision we take in the current stage
q_i^k is the single-state return resulting from taking decision k in state i.

In successively evaluating the $f_n(.)$ we need storage locations in the computer for $\{f_{n-1}(j)\}$, $\{f_n(i)\}$ and $\{k_n^*(i)\}$, the optimal decision for state i at stage n. Consequently if there are N states altogether we would need 3N words of computer storage, apart from those required to store the program itself. Also, in order to backtrack after $f_N(.)$ has been evaluated, we would need all the $k_n^*(.)$ for all the stages. Thus the number of words of storage required is of the same order as the number of states. In the examples dealt with so far this would have caused no problem. It is very easy, however, to think of examples of dynamic programming which it would be very difficult to solve on a computer.

Example: inventory problem

Suppose we are concerned with an inventory control problem in which there are ten products which use common production facilities, so that their inventory policies are interdependent. It would be natural to think of this problem in dynamic programming terms and to consider a ten-dimensional state description $(I_1, I_2, \ldots I_{10})$ where I_m is the inventory level of product m at stage n. If the inventory of each product could have one of eight values (from 0 to 7, for example), then it would be natural again to define $f_n(I_1, I_2, \ldots I_{10})$ as the expected cost associated with having inventory levels I_m of product m (m = 1 to 10) and proceeding optimally over the next n periods.

It is disconcerting to reckon the number of states. Each product can have any of 8 levels and the states can be anything from 0000000000 to 7777777777, so that there are 8^{10} states in all, far too many for their state-values to be stored conveniently on even the largest computer. Yet this is not a particularly artificial problem: ten products is not very many and a maximal inventory of 7 for each product is very low.

Conclusion

In examples of this type the number of states is given by the number of values each variable can take to the power of the number of variables. Of these two numbers it is the number of variables which is the more restricting from the computational point of view, since it is often possible to use a coarser grid size to reduce the number of values each variable can take. Thus if there are M variables and each can take S levels, the total number of states is S^M. Doubling the number of levels increases the number of states by a factor 2^M, whereas doubling the number of variables increases the number of states by a factor S^M. The number of variables in the state description, known as the dimensionality, is one of the biggest stumbling blocks in the widespread use of dynamic programming and much ingenuity has been used to get over it.

4.2 Lagrange Multipliers

Overview

A suggestion frequently made for overcoming the "curse of dimensionality" is the use of Lagrange multipliers; however they are of limited applicability. It must be emphasized that the sufficient condition for the successful use of Lagrange multipliers may not hold; this section illustrates their unsuccessful use.

Example: loading a barge

We consider a more complex variant of the barge problem.

Suppose that the cargo which can be loaded in the barge is limited not only by weight (C = 100 tons) but by volume (V = 20 cubic yards) and that a package of type n has not only a weight w_n but also a volume s_n. To fix ideas, let the value, weight and volume of a single package of each of the n types be as follows:

Package type (n)	*Value per package (v_n)*	*Weight per package (w_n)*	*Volume per package (s_n)*
1	42	40	8
2	26	30	3
3	11	15	2
4	7	8	3

With an obvious extension to the original formulation, we may define $f_n(W,S)$ as the value associated with having a weight of W tons and a volume of S cubic yards available for loading with packages of the first n types, using an optimal policy. Again, optimal means greatest value.

The transition rules are that each package of type n loaded will reduce the weight W and volume S available for loading by w_n and s_n respectively, so we may write

$$f_n(W,S) = \max_{\substack{0 \leqslant x_n \leqslant \left[\frac{W}{w_n}\right] \\ 0 \leqslant x_n \leqslant \left[\frac{S}{s_n}\right]}} \Big(x_n v_n + f_{n-1}(W - x_n w_n, S - x_n s_n)\Big), n \geqslant 2$$

and
$$f_1(W,S) = \max_{\substack{0 \leqslant x_1 \leqslant \left[\frac{W}{w_1}\right] \\ 0 \leqslant x_1 \leqslant \left[\frac{S}{s_1}\right]}} (x_1 v_1)$$

As before, we could compute $f_1(W,S)$, $f_2(W,S)$ and so on successively for values of W from 0 to 100 in stages of 5 and for values of S from 0 to 20 in stages of 1, although in the present case, in recording the state values and the optimal decisions at each stage, we shall have a series of two-way tables (Tables 4.1 to 4.8) for various values of W and S.

The tables show successive values of $f_n^*(W,S)$ and the associated decisions $x_n^*(W,S)$, for values of S from 0 to 22, so that the optimal loading policy found in Section 2.1 (p. 26) can be confirmed. This policy has a value of 98, resulting from loading two packages of type 1 and two packages of type 4. The total weight is 98 tons (within the capacity constraint of 100 tons), but the total volume is 22 cubic yards (in excess of the capacity constraint of 20 cubic yards). The optimal loading policy for a capacity constraint of 20 cubic yards is to load 2 packages of type 1 and 1 package of type 3 with a value of 95 and a total weight of 95 tons.

$\{f_1(W,S)\}$

	0	1	2	3	4	5	6	7	8	9	10	11	12	13	14	15	16	17	18	19	20	21	22
0	0	0	0	0	0	0	0	0	0	0	0	0	0	0	0	0	0	0	0	0	0	0	0
5	0	0	0	0	0	0	0	0	0	0	0	0	0	0	0	0	0	0	0	0	0	0	0
10	0	0	0	0	0	0	0	0	0	0	0	0	0	0	0	0	0	0	0	0	0	0	0
15	0	0	0	0	0	0	0	0	0	0	0	0	0	0	0	0	0	0	0	0	0	0	0
20	0	0	0	0	0	0	0	0	0	0	0	0	0	0	0	0	0	0	0	0	0	0	0
25	0	0	0	0	0	0	0	0	0	0	0	0	0	0	0	0	0	0	0	0	0	0	0
30	0	0	0	0	0	0	0	0	0	0	0	0	0	0	0	0	0	0	0	0	0	0	0
35	0	0	0	0	0	0	0	0	0	0	0	0	0	0	0	0	0	0	0	0	0	0	0
40	0	0	0	0	0	0	0	0	42	42	42	42	42	42	42	42	42	42	42	42	42	42	42
45	0	0	0	0	0	0	0	0	42	42	42	42	42	42	42	42	42	42	42	42	42	42	42
50	0	0	0	0	0	0	0	0	42	42	42	42	42	42	42	42	42	42	42	42	42	42	42
55	0	0	0	0	0	0	0	0	42	42	42	42	42	42	42	42	42	42	42	42	42	42	42
60	0	0	0	0	0	0	0	0	42	42	42	42	42	42	42	42	42	42	42	42	42	42	42
65	0	0	0	0	0	0	0	0	42	42	42	42	42	42	42	42	42	42	42	42	42	42	42
70	0	0	0	0	0	0	0	0	42	42	42	42	42	42	42	42	42	42	42	42	42	42	42
75	0	0	0	0	0	0	0	0	42	42	42	42	42	42	42	42	42	42	42	42	42	42	42
80	0	0	0	0	0	0	0	0	42	42	42	42	42	42	42	42	84	84	84	84	84	84	84
85	0	0	0	0	0	0	0	0	42	42	42	42	42	42	42	42	84	84	84	84	84	84	84
90	0	0	0	0	0	0	0	0	42	42	42	42	42	42	42	42	84	84	84	84	84	84	84
95	0	0	0	0	0	0	0	0	42	42	42	42	42	42	42	42	84	84	84	84	84	84	84
100	0	0	0	0	0	0	0	0	42	42	42	42	42	42	42	42	84	84	84	84	84	84	84

Table 4.1

$\{f_2(W,S)\}$

	0	1	2	3	4	5	6	7	8	9	10	11	12	13	14	15	16	17	18	19	20	21	22
0	0	0	0	0	0	0	0	0	0	0	0	0	0	0	0	0	0	0	0	0	0	0	0
5	0	0	0	0	0	0	0	0	0	0	0	0	0	0	0	0	0	0	0	0	0	0	0
10	0	0	0	0	0	0	0	0	0	0	0	0	0	0	0	0	0	0	0	0	0	0	0
15	0	0	0	0	0	0	0	0	0	0	0	0	0	0	0	0	0	0	0	0	0	0	0
20	0	0	0	0	0	0	0	0	0	0	0	0	0	0	0	0	0	0	0	0	0	0	0
25	0	0	0	0	0	0	0	0	0	0	0	0	0	0	0	0	0	0	0	0	0	0	0
30	0	0	0	26	26	26	26	26	26	26	26	26	26	26	26	26	26	26	26	26	26	26	26
35	0	0	0	26	26	26	26	26	26	26	26	26	26	26	26	26	26	26	26	26	26	26	26
40	0	0	0	26	26	26	26	26	42	42	42	42	42	42	42	42	42	42	42	42	42	42	42
45	0	0	0	26	26	26	26	26	42	42	42	42	42	42	42	42	42	42	42	42	42	42	42
50	0	0	0	26	26	26	26	26	42	42	42	42	42	42	42	42	42	42	42	42	42	42	42
55	0	0	0	26	26	26	26	26	42	42	42	42	42	42	42	42	42	42	42	42	42	42	42
60	0	0	0	26	26	26	52	52	52	52	52	52	52	52	52	52	52	52	52	52	52	52	52
65	0	0	0	26	26	26	52	52	52	52	52	52	52	52	52	52	52	52	52	52	52	52	52
70	0	0	0	26	26	26	52	52	52	52	52	68	68	68	68	68	68	68	68	68	68	68	68
75	0	0	0	26	26	26	52	52	52	52	52	68	68	68	68	68	68	68	68	68	68	68	68
80	0	0	0	26	26	26	52	52	52	52	52	68	68	68	68	68	84	84	84	84	84	84	84
85	0	0	0	26	26	26	52	52	52	52	52	68	68	68	68	68	84	84	84	84	84	84	84
90	0	0	0	26	26	26	52	52	52	78	78	78	78	78	78	78	84	84	84	84	84	84	84
95	0	0	0	26	26	26	52	52	52	78	78	78	78	78	78	78	84	84	84	84	84	84	84
100	0	0	0	26	26	26	52	52	52	78	78	78	78	78	94	94	94	94	94	94	94	94	94

Table 4.2

$\{f_3(W,S)\}$

	0	1	2	3	4	5	6	7	8	9	10	11	12	13	14	15	16	17	18	19	20	21	22
0	0	0	0	0	0	0	0	0	0	0	0	0	0	0	0	0	0	0	0	0	0	0	0
5	0	0	0	0	0	0	0	0	0	0	0	0	0	0	0	0	0	0	0	0	0	0	0
10	0	0	0	0	0	0	0	0	0	0	0	0	0	0	0	0	0	0	0	0	0	0	0
15	0	0	11	11	11	11	11	11	11	11	11	11	11	11	11	11	11	11	11	11	11	11	11
20	0	0	11	11	11	11	11	11	11	11	11	11	11	11	11	11	11	11	11	11	11	11	11
25	0	0	11	11	11	11	11	11	11	11	11	11	11	11	11	11	11	11	11	11	11	11	11
30	0	0	11	26	26	26	26	26	26	26	26	26	26	26	26	26	26	26	26	26	26	26	26
35	0	0	11	26	26	26	26	26	26	26	26	26	26	26	26	26	26	26	26	26	26	26	26
40	0	0	11	26	26	26	26	26	42	42	42	42	42	42	42	42	42	42	42	42	42	42	42
45	0	0	11	26	26	37	37	37	42	42	42	42	42	42	42	42	42	42	42	42	42	42	42
50	0	0	11	26	26	37	37	37	42	42	42	42	42	42	42	42	42	42	42	42	42	42	42
55	0	0	11	26	26	37	37	37	42	42	53	53	53	53	53	53	53	53	53	53	53	53	53
60	0	0	11	26	26	37	52	52	52	52	53	53	53	53	53	53	53	53	53	53	53	53	53
65	0	0	11	26	26	37	52	52	52	52	53	53	53	53	53	53	53	53	53	53	53	53	53
70	0	0	11	26	26	37	52	52	52	52	53	68	68	68	68	68	68	68	68	68	68	68	68
75	0	0	11	26	26	37	52	52	63	63	63	68	68	68	68	68	68	68	68	68	68	68	68
80	0	0	11	26	26	37	52	52	63	63	63	68	68	68	68	68	84	84	84	84	84	84	84
85	0	0	11	26	26	37	52	52	63	63	63	68	68	79	79	79	84	84	84	84	84	84	84
90	0	0	11	26	26	37	52	52	63	78	78	78	78	79	79	79	84	84	84	84	84	84	84
95	0	0	11	26	26	37	52	52	63	78	78	78	78	79	79	79	84	84	95	95	95	95	95
100	0	0	11	26	26	37	52	52	63	78	78	78	78	79	94	94	94	94	95	95	95	95	95

Table 4.3

$\{f_4(W,S)\}$

	0	1	2	3	4	5	6	7	8	9	10	11	12	13	14	15	16	17	18	19	20	21	22
0	0	0	0	0	0	0	0	0	0	0	0	0	0	0	0	0	0	0	0	0	0	0	0
5	0	0	0	0	0	0	0	0	0	0	0	0	0	0	0	0	0	0	0	0	0	0	0
10	0	0	0	7	7	7	7	7	7	7	7	7	7	7	7	7	7	7	7	7	7	7	7
15	0	0	11	11	11	11	11	11	11	11	11	11	11	11	11	11	11	11	11	11	11	11	11
20	0	0	11	11	11	11	14	14	14	14	14	14	14	14	14	14	14	14	14	14	14	14	14
25	0	0	11	11	11	18	18	18	18	21	21	21	21	21	21	21	21	21	21	21	21	21	21
30	0	0	11	26	26	26	26	26	26	26	26	26	26	26	26	26	26	26	26	26	26	26	26
35	0	0	11	26	26	26	26	26	26	26	26	28	28	28	28	28	28	28	28	28	28	28	28
40	0	0	11	26	26	26	33	33	42	42	42	42	42	42	42	42	42	42	42	42	42	42	42
45	0	0	11	26	26	37	37	37	42	42	42	42	42	42	42	42	42	42	42	42	42	42	42
50	0	0	11	26	26	37	37	37	42	42	42	49	49	49	49	49	49	49	49	49	49	49	49
55	0	0	11	26	26	37	37	37	44	44	53	53	53	53	53	53	53	53	53	53	53	53	53
60	0	0	11	26	26	37	52	52	52	52	53	53	53	53	56	56	56	56	56	56	56	56	56
65	0	0	11	26	26	37	52	52	52	52	53	53	53	60	60	60	60	63	63	63	63	63	63
70	0	0	11	26	26	37	52	52	52	59	59	68	68	68	68	68	68	68	68	68	68	68	68
75	0	0	11	26	26	37	52	52	63	63	63	68	68	68	68	68	68	68	68	68	70	70	70
80	0	0	11	26	26	37	52	52	63	63	63	68	68	68	75	75	84	84	84	84	84	84	84
85	0	0	11	26	26	37	52	52	63	63	63	70	70	79	79	79	84	84	84	84	84	84	84
90	0	0	11	26	26	37	52	52	63	78	78	78	78	79	79	79	84	84	84	91	91	91	91
95	0	0	11	26	26	37	52	52	63	78	78	78	78	79	79	79	86	86	95	95	95	95	95
100	0	0	11	26	26	37	52	52	63	78	78	78	85	85	94	94	94	94	95	95	95	95	98

Table 4.4

$\left\{x_1^*(W,S)\right\}$

	0	1	2	3	4	5	6	7	8	9	10	11	12	13	14	15	16	17	18	19	20	21	22
0	0	0	0	0	0	0	0	0	0	0	0	0	0	0	0	0	0	0	0	0	0	0	0
5	0	0	0	0	0	0	0	0	0	0	0	0	0	0	0	0	0	0	0	0	0	0	0
10	0	0	0	0	0	0	0	0	0	0	0	0	0	0	0	0	0	0	0	0	0	0	0
15	0	0	0	0	0	0	0	0	0	0	0	0	0	0	0	0	0	0	0	0	0	0	0
20	0	0	0	0	0	0	0	0	0	0	0	0	0	0	0	0	0	0	0	0	0	0	0
25	0	0	0	0	0	0	0	0	0	0	0	0	0	0	0	0	0	0	0	0	0	0	0
30	0	0	0	0	0	0	0	0	0	0	0	0	0	0	0	0	0	0	0	0	0	0	0
35	0	0	0	0	0	0	0	0	0	0	0	0	0	0	0	0	0	0	0	0	0	0	0
40	0	0	0	0	0	0	0	0	1	1	1	1	1	1	1	1	1	1	1	1	1	1	1
45	0	0	0	0	0	0	0	0	1	1	1	1	1	1	1	1	1	1	1	1	1	1	1
50	0	0	0	0	0	0	0	0	1	1	1	1	1	1	1	1	1	1	1	1	1	1	1
55	0	0	0	0	0	0	0	0	1	1	1	1	1	1	1	1	1	1	1	1	1	1	1
60	0	0	0	0	0	0	0	0	1	1	1	1	1	1	1	1	1	1	1	1	1	1	1
65	0	0	0	0	0	0	0	0	1	1	1	1	1	1	1	1	1	1	1	1	1	1	1
70	0	0	0	0	0	0	0	0	1	1	1	1	1	1	1	1	1	1	1	1	1	1	1
75	0	0	0	0	0	0	0	0	1	1	1	1	1	1	1	1	1	1	1	1	1	1	1
80	0	0	0	0	0	0	0	0	1	1	1	1	1	1	1	1	2	2	2	2	2	2	2
85	0	0	0	0	0	0	0	0	1	1	1	1	1	1	1	1	2	2	2	2	2	2	2
90	0	0	0	0	0	0	0	0	1	1	1	1	1	1	1	1	2	2	2	2	2	2	2
95	0	0	0	0	0	0	0	0	1	1	1	1	1	1	1	1	2	2	2	2	2	2	2
100	0	0	0	0	0	0	0	0	1	1	1	1	1	1	1	1	2	2	2	2	2	2	2

Table 4.5

$\left\{x_2^*(W,S)\right\}$

	0	1	2	3	4	5	6	7	8	9	10	11	12	13	14	15	16	17	18	19	20	21	22
0	0	0	0	0	0	0	0	0	0	0	0	0	0	0	0	0	0	0	0	0	0	0	0
5	0	0	0	0	0	0	0	0	0	0	0	0	0	0	0	0	0	0	0	0	0	0	0
10	0	0	0	0	0	0	0	0	0	0	0	0	0	0	0	0	0	0	0	0	0	0	0
15	0	0	0	0	0	0	0	0	0	0	0	0	0	0	0	0	0	0	0	0	0	0	0
20	0	0	0	0	0	0	0	0	0	0	0	0	0	0	0	0	0	0	0	0	0	0	0
25	0	0	0	0	0	0	0	0	0	0	0	0	0	0	0	0	0	0	0	0	0	0	0
30	0	0	0	1	1	1	1	1	1	1	1	1	1	1	1	1	1	1	1	1	1	1	1
35	0	0	0	1	1	1	1	1	1	1	1	1	1	1	1	1	1	1	1	1	1	1	1
40	0	0	0	1	1	1	1	1	0	0	0	0	0	0	0	0	0	0	0	0	0	0	0
45	0	0	0	1	1	1	1	1	0	0	0	0	0	0	0	0	0	0	0	0	0	0	0
50	0	0	0	1	1	1	1	1	0	0	0	0	0	0	0	0	0	0	0	0	0	0	0
55	0	0	0	1	1	1	1	1	0	0	0	0	0	0	0	0	0	0	0	0	0	0	0
60	0	0	0	1	1	1	2	2	2	2	2	2	2	2	2	2	2	2	2	2	2	2	2
65	0	0	0	1	1	1	2	2	2	2	2	2	2	2	2	2	2	2	2	2	2	2	2
70	0	0	0	1	1	1	2	2	2	2	2	1	1	1	1	1	1	1	1	1	1	1	1
75	0	0	0	1	1	1	2	2	2	2	2	1	1	1	1	1	1	1	1	1	1	1	1
80	0	0	0	1	1	1	2	2	2	2	2	1	1	1	1	1	0	0	0	0	0	0	0
85	0	0	0	1	1	1	2	2	2	2	2	1	1	1	1	1	0	0	0	0	0	0	0
90	0	0	0	1	1	1	2	2	2	3	3	3	3	3	3	3	0	0	0	0	0	0	0
95	0	0	0	1	1	1	2	2	2	3	3	3	3	3	3	3	0	0	0	0	0	0	0
100	0	0	0	1	1	1	2	2	2	3	3	3	3	3	2	2	2	2	2	2	2	2	2

Table 4.6

$\left\{x_3^*(W,S)\right\}$

	0	1	2	3	4	5	6	7	8	9	10	11	12	13	14	15	16	17	18	19	20	21	22
0	0	0	0	0	0	0	0	0	0	0	0	0	0	0	0	0	0	0	0	0	0	0	0
5	0	0	0	0	0	0	0	0	0	0	0	0	0	0	0	0	0	0	0	0	0	0	0
10	0	0	0	0	0	0	0	0	0	0	0	0	0	0	0	0	0	0	0	0	0	0	0
15	0	0	1	1	1	1	1	1	1	1	1	1	1	1	1	1	1	1	1	1	1	1	1
20	0	0	1	1	1	1	1	1	1	1	1	1	1	1	1	1	1	1	1	1	1	1	1
25	0	0	1	1	1	1	1	1	1	1	1	1	1	1	1	1	1	1	1	1	1	1	1
30	0	0	1	0	0	0	0	0	0	0	0	0	0	0	0	0	0	0	0	0	0	0	0
35	0	0	1	0	0	0	0	0	0	0	0	0	0	0	0	0	0	0	0	0	0	0	0
40	0	0	1	0	0	0	0	0	0	0	0	0	0	0	0	0	0	0	0	0	0	0	0
45	0	0	1	0	0	1	1	1	0	0	0	0	0	0	0	0	0	0	0	0	0	0	0
50	0	0	1	0	0	1	1	1	0	0	0	0	0	0	0	0	0	0	0	0	0	0	0
55	0	0	1	0	0	1	1	1	0	0	1	1	1	1	1	1	1	1	1	1	1	1	1
60	0	0	1	0	0	1	0	0	0	0	1	1	1	1	1	1	1	1	1	1	1	1	1
65	0	0	1	0	0	1	0	0	0	0	1	1	1	1	1	1	1	1	1	1	1	1	1
70	0	0	1	0	0	1	0	0	0	0	1	0	0	0	0	0	0	0	0	0	0	0	0
75	0	0	1	0	0	1	0	0	1	1	1	0	0	0	0	0	0	0	0	0	0	0	0
80	0	0	1	0	0	1	0	0	1	1	1	0	0	0	0	0	0	0	0	0	0	0	0
85	0	0	1	0	0	1	0	0	1	1	1	0	0	1	1	1	0	0	0	0	0	0	0
90	0	0	1	0	0	1	0	0	1	0	0	0	0	1	1	1	0	0	0	0	0	0	0
95	0	0	1	0	0	1	0	0	1	0	0	0	0	1	1	1	0	0	1	1	1	1	1
100	0	0	1	0	0	1	0	0	1	0	0	0	0	1	0	0	0	0	1	1	1	1	1

Table 4.7

$\left\{x_4^*(W,S)\right\}$

	0	1	2	3	4	5	6	7	8	9	10	11	12	13	14	15	16	17	18	19	20	21	22
0	0	0	0	0	0	0	0	0	0	0	0	0	0	0	0	0	0	0	0	0	0	0	0
5	0	0	0	0	0	0	0	0	0	0	0	0	0	0	0	0	0	0	0	0	0	0	0
10	0	0	0	1	1	1	1	1	1	1	1	1	1	1	1	1	1	1	1	1	1	1	1
15	0	0	0	0	0	0	0	0	0	0	0	0	0	0	0	0	0	0	0	0	0	0	0
20	0	0	0	0	0	0	2	2	2	2	2	2	2	2	2	2	2	2	2	2	2	2	2
25	0	0	0	0	0	1	1	1	1	3	3	3	3	3	3	3	3	3	3	3	3	3	3
30	0	0	0	0	0	0	0	0	0	0	0	0	0	0	0	0	0	0	0	0	0	0	0
35	0	0	0	0	0	0	0	0	0	0	0	0	4	4	4	4	4	4	4	4	4	4	4
40	0	0	0	0	0	0	1	1	0	0	0	0	0	0	0	0	0	0	0	0	0	0	0
45	0	0	0	0	0	0	0	0	0	0	0	0	0	0	0	0	0	0	0	0	0	0	0
50	0	0	0	0	0	0	0	0	0	0	0	1	1	1	1	1	1	1	1	1	1	1	1
55	0	0	0	0	0	0	0	0	1	1	0	0	0	0	0	0	0	0	0	0	0	0	0
60	0	0	0	0	0	0	0	0	0	0	0	0	0	0	2	2	2	2	2	2	2	2	2
65	0	0	0	0	0	0	0	0	0	0	0	0	0	1	1	1	1	3	3	3	3	3	3
70	0	0	0	0	0	0	0	0	0	1	1	0	0	0	0	0	0	0	0	0	0	0	0
75	0	0	0	0	0	0	0	0	0	0	0	0	0	0	0	0	0	0	0	0	4	4	4
80	0	0	0	0	0	0	0	0	0	0	0	0	0	0	1	1	0	0	0	0	0	0	0
85	0	0	0	0	0	0	0	0	0	0	0	1	1	0	0	0	0	0	0	0	0	0	0
90	0	0	0	0	0	0	0	0	0	0	0	0	0	0	0	0	0	0	0	1	1	1	1
95	0	0	0	0	0	0	0	0	0	0	0	0	0	0	0	0	1	1	0	0	0	0	0
100	0	0	0	0	0	0	0	0	0	0	0	0	1	1	0	0	0	0	0	0	0	0	2

Table 4.8

The computational labour, while not heavy, is not trivial; this problem with its two-dimensional state description might seem a suitable one for solution by the use of Lagrange multipliers. In this example the procedure is to solve a series of one-dimensional problems concerned (for instance) with weight alone by subtracting from the value of each package an imputed cost proportional to its volume. If we call this imputed cost per unit of volume λ, then the revised values of each package type will be

Type	*Revised value*
1	$42 - 8\lambda$
2	$26 - 3\lambda$
3	$11 - 2\lambda$
4	$7 - 3\lambda$

and the problem now has the same formulation as that posed in Section 2.1. If $\lambda = 0$, the revised values are the same as the old values and the solution will be the same as we obtained in Section 2.1 and as shown in the right-hand columns of Tables 4.4 and 4.8. The greater the value of λ, the greater the imputed cost of volume and the less the total volume of that combination of packages which will maximize the total revised value of the cargo subject to the 100-ton weight constraint. For example, if $\lambda = 5\frac{1}{2}$, then it would be worthwhile loading only packages of type 2, since only type 2 packages would have a positive revised value. In this case we would load three packages of type 2, for a total revised value of $28\frac{1}{2}$ ($= 3 \times (26 - 3\lambda)$), a total weight of 90 and a total volume of 9 cubic yards. For some particular value of λ, somewhere between 0 and $5\frac{1}{2}$, we hope to hit on an optimal loading schedule which will have a total volume of 20 cubic yards and a total weight of not more than 100 tons.

Suppose we take $\lambda = 3$, with weights and revised values as follows:

n	w_n	v_n^*
1	40	18
2	30	17
3	15	5
4	8	−2

It is straightforward to derive Table 4.9 for $f_3(W)$ and $x_3^*(W)$. (Clearly there is no point in loading any packages of type 4).

Thus for $\lambda = 3$ we would load 2 packages of type 2 and 1 package of type 1 for a total (revised) value of 52, a total weight of 100 and a total volume of 14 cubic yards. If we were to take $\lambda = 2$ and $\lambda = 1$ we would

$\lambda = 3$

W	$f_1(W)$	$x_1^*(W)$	$f_2(W)$	$x_2^*(W)$	$f_3(W)$	$x_3^*(W)$
100	36	2	52	2	52	0
95	36	2	51	3		
90	36	2	51	3		
85	36	2	36	0		
80	36	2	36	0		
75	18	1	35	1		
70	18	1	35	1		
65	18	1	34	2		
60	18	1	34	2		
55	18	1	18	0		
50	18	1	18	0		
45	18	1	18	0		
40	18	1	18	0		
35	0	0	17	1		
30	0	0	17	1		
25	0	0	0	0		
20	0	0	0	0		
15	0	0	0	0		
10	0	0	0	0		
5	0	0	0	0		

Table 4.9

(so it turns out) hit on exactly the same policy. For $\lambda = \frac{1}{2}$ we discover two policies equally good: one of them is the one which is optimal for $\lambda = 1,2,3$ and the other is the one which is optimal for $\lambda = 0$. Table 4.10 is the relevant table of $\{f_n(W)\}$ and $\{x_n^*(W)\}$.

$\lambda = \frac{1}{2}$

W	$f_1(W)$	$x_1^*(W)$	$f_2(W)$	$x_2^*(W)$	$f_3(W)$	$x_3^*(W)$	$f_4(W)$	$x_4^*(W)$
100	76	2	87	2	87	0	87	0 or 2
95	76	2	76	0	86	1		
90	76	2	76	0	76	0		
85	76	2	76	0	76	0		
80	76	2	76	0	76	0		
75	38	1	$62\frac{1}{2}$	1	$62\frac{1}{2}$	0		
70	38	1	$62\frac{1}{2}$	1	$62\frac{1}{2}$	0		
65	38	1	49	2	49	0		
60	38	1	49	2	49	0		
55	38	1	38	0	48	1		
50	38	1	38	0	38	0		
45	38	1	38	0	38	0		
40	38	1	38	0	38	0		
35	0	0	$24\frac{1}{2}$	1	$24\frac{1}{2}$	0		
30	0	0	$24\frac{1}{2}$	1	$24\frac{1}{2}$	0		
25	0	0	0	0	10	1		
20	0	0	0	0	10	1		
15	0	0	0	0	10	1		
10	0	0	0	0	0	0		
5	0	0	0	0	0	0		

Table 4.10

It appears reasonable that we should write out Table 4.11 (we shall confirm below the changeover value of $\lambda = 3\frac{1}{5}$).

Range of λ	n 1 2 3 4	Value	Weight	Volume
$0 \leqslant \lambda \leqslant \frac{1}{2}$	2 0 0 2	98	96	22
$\frac{1}{2} \leqslant \lambda \leqslant 3\frac{1}{5}$	1 2 0 0	94	100	14
$3\frac{1}{5} \leqslant \lambda \leqslant 5\frac{1}{2}$	0 3 0 0	78	90	9

Table 4.11

If these results are compared with the tables of $\{f_n(W,S)\}$ and $\{x_n^*(W,S)\}$ earlier in this section, they will be seen to agree in part with the results already obtained: the values of $f_4(100,22)$, $f_4(100,14)$ and $f_4(100,9)$ all check with the respective elements in the bottom row of the $\{f_4(W,S)\}$ table (Table 4.4). What is odd is that even though we have varied λ over all sensible values (from $\lambda = 0$ where there is no imputed storage cost, to $\lambda = 5\frac{1}{2}$ where it only makes sense to load packages of one type only), we have not found the optimal loading policy for a barge which can take 20 cubic feet of cargo. We know the value of $f_4(100,20)$ because we have already worked it out: why do we not come across it by varying λ?

The reason is that there is no guarantee that by varying λ all the optimal policies for different volume constraints will be discovered. The three optimal policies given in the previous table are the result of taking values of λ over a variety of ranges, λ representing an imputed cost per unit of volume. Thus at the value of λ at which the first two policies are both optimal,

$$98 - 22\lambda = 94 - 14\lambda$$

$$\text{and} \quad \lambda = \tfrac{1}{2}$$

Similarly at the value of λ at which the second and third policies are both optimal,

$$94 - 14\lambda = 78 - 9\lambda$$

$$\text{and} \quad \lambda = 3\tfrac{1}{5}$$

From previous calculations of $f_4(100,20)$ we know that the optimal way to load a barge which can take up to 100 tons and 20 cubic feet is to carry one package of type 3 and two packages of type 1 with a total value of 95, a total weight of 100 tons and a total volume of 18. The revised value of this load is $95 - 18\lambda$ and this quantity is never greater than whichever is the greatest of the quantities $98 - 22\lambda$, $94 - 14\lambda$ and $78 - 9\lambda$. This is shown in Figure 4.1 in which are plotted all the revised values of the optimal loading policies for various cargo volumes.

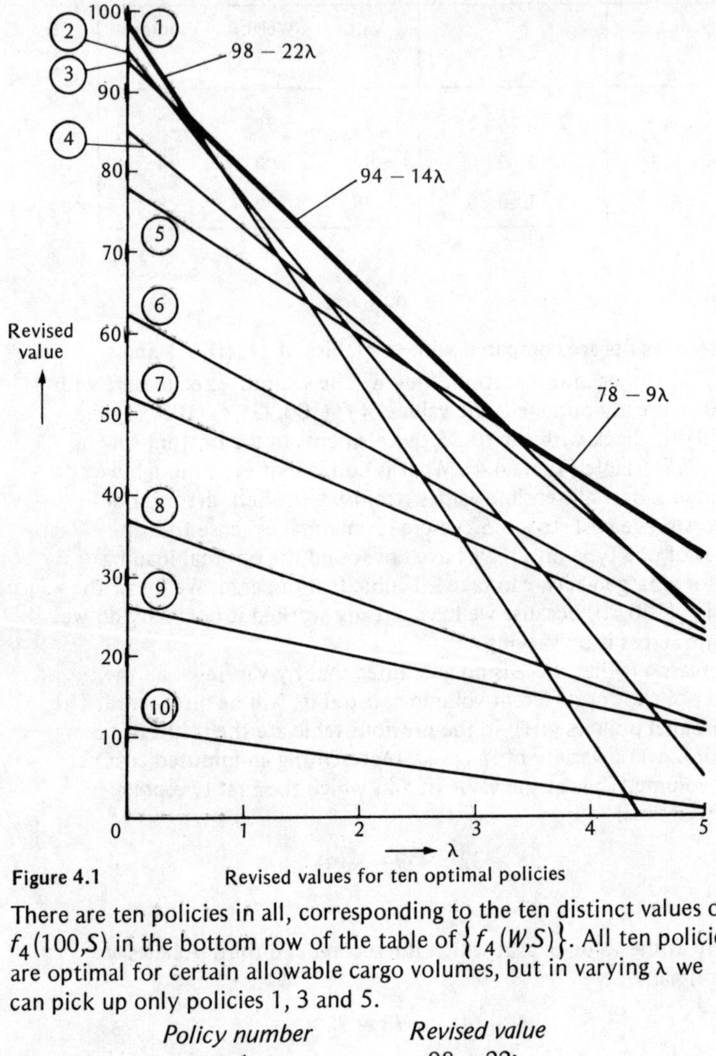

Figure 4.1 Revised values for ten optimal policies

There are ten policies in all, corresponding to the ten distinct values of $f_4(100,S)$ in the bottom row of the table of $\{f_4(W,S)\}$. All ten policies are optimal for certain allowable cargo volumes, but in varying λ we can pick up only policies 1, 3 and 5.

Policy number	*Revised value*
1	98 − 22λ
2	95 − 18λ
3	94 − 14λ
4	85 − 12λ
5	78 − 9λ
6	63 − 8λ
7	52 − 6λ
8	37 − 5λ
9	26 − 3λ
10	11 − 2λ

Conclusion

Great care needs to be taken in using the Lagrange multipliers to ensure that optimal policies are not missed: unless by varying λ we can find a solution which satisfies the constraint exactly we cannot take it for granted that one of the solutions which has been determined must be optimal. In practice, we might possibly try to find the second best, third best, fourth best policy, and so on until the constraint is satisfied exactly, but the derivation of these policies is not trivial. Consequently the power of Lagrange multipliers in reducing the burden of dimensionality is limited.

4.3 Grid Size

Overview

The aim of Lagrange multipliers is to reduce a dynamic programming problem to a smaller problem in which the state description has at least one less dimension. In practice, it is always worthwhile experimenting to see if the dimensionality needs to be reduced at all: it may be that a sufficiently accurate solution can be found by preserving all the dimensions in the state description, but considering fewer values in each dimension.

Example: loading a barge

Suppose that we have a deterministic problem of two dimensions (such as the barge problem). We may in principle write down its functional equation as

$$f_n(x,y) = \max_k \left[q^k_{x,y} + f_{n-1}(x',y') \right]$$

Each time we need to compute the optimal decision k, at the nth stage, for the state (x,y) we need the already computed value $f_{n-1}(x',y')$, where $(x'y')$ is the transformed state resulting from taking decision k at state (x,y). We can show all the values of $f_{n-1}(x',y')$ in a two-way table (see Table 4.12).

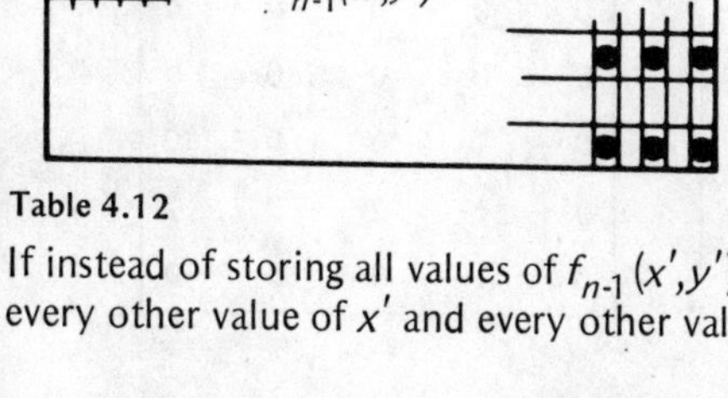

Table 4.12

If instead of storing all values of $f_{n-1}(x',y')$ we stored values for only every other value of x' and every other value of y', we would reduce storage requirements for the $f_{n-1}(x',y')$ values by four times. If this results in a policy which is close to the optimal policy, it may be judged worthwhile.

For example, in the barge problem we could have computed values of $f_n(W,S)$ for values of W from 0 to 100 by 1. Instead, we lost nothing (because of the package weights being multiples of 5 tons, with one exception) by taking values of W from 0 to 100 by 5. We lost nothing in terms of accuracy and in terms of efficiency we reduced the computational load by almost 80%.

If we took a grid size of 10 tons and 2 cubic yards, then the differen in the solution would be very small. In fact (as the interested reader may verify) there would be only three entries in the final tables which would be different, namely

$$f_4(40,6) = 26,\ x_4^* = 0$$
$$f_4(80,14) = 68,\ x_4^* = 0$$
$$f_4(100,12) = 78,\ x_4^* = 0$$

and again the computational load would have been reduced, this time by almost three-quarters.

Obviously the grid size can be made so coarse that the solutions are further away from the optimal policy. For example, a grid of 25 tons and 5 cubic yards in the barge problem would give rise to the computational results in Table 4.13, (i) to (viii).

(i) $\{f_1(W,S)\}$

W \ S	0	5	10	15	20
0	0	0	0	0	0
25	0	0	0	0	0
50	0	0	42	42	42
75	0	0	42	42	42
100	0	0	42	42	84

(ii) $\{x_1^*(W,S)\}$

0	0	0	0	0
0	0	0	0	0
0	0	1	1	1
0	0	1	1	1
0	0	1	1	2

(iii) $\{f_2(W,S)\}$

W \ S	0	5	10	15	20
0	0	0	0	0	0
25	0	0	0	0	0
50	0	26	42	42	42
75	0	26	52	52	52
100	0	26	78	78	84

(iv) $\{x_2^*(W,S)\}$

0	0	0	0	0
0	0	0	0	0
0	1	0	0	0
0	1	2	2	2
0	1	3	3	0

(v) $\{f_3(W,S)\}$

W \ S	0	5	10	15	20
0	0	0	0	0	0
25	0	11	11	11	11
50	0	26	42	42	42
75	0	26	52	53	53
100	0	26	78	78	84

(vi) $\{x_3^*(W,S)\}$

0	0	0	0	0
0	1	1	1	1
0	0	0	0	0
0	0	0	1	1
0	0	0	0	0

(vii) $\{f_4(W,S)\}$

W \ S	0	5	10	15	20
0	0	0	0	0	0
25	0	11	21	21	21
50	0	26	42	42	42
75	0	26	52	53	63
100	0	26	78	78	84

(viii) $\{x_4^*(W,S)\}$

0	0	0	0	0
0	0	3	3	3
0	0	0	0	0
0	0	0	0	3
0	0	0	0	0

Table 4.13

To illustrate the computation, we note that

$$f_4(75,20) = \max\begin{bmatrix} x=0: & 0+f_3(75,20) \\ x=1: & 7+f_3(67,17) \\ x=2: & 14+f_3(59,14) \\ x=3: & 21+f_3(51,11) \end{bmatrix}$$

$$= \max\begin{bmatrix} 0+f_3(75,20) \\ 7+f_3(50,15) \\ 14+f_3(50,10) \\ 21+f_3(50,10) \end{bmatrix}$$

$$= \max\begin{bmatrix} 0+53 \\ 7+42 \\ 14+42 \\ 21+42 \end{bmatrix} \leftarrow$$

$$= 63 \text{ and } x_4^*(75,20) = 3$$

Parts (vii) and (viii) of Table 4.13 may be compared with the relevant entries in the tables derived for the complete problem, Table 4.14, (i) and (ii). It may be seen that the correspondence, though by no means close, is not remote even with such a crude grid size.

(i) $\{f_4(W,S)\}$

0	0	0	0	0
0	18	21	21	21
0	37	42	49	49
0	37	63	68	70
0	37	78	94	95

(ii) $\{x_4^*(W,S)\}$

0	0	0	0	0
0	1	3	3	3
0	0	0	1	1
0	0	0	0	4
0	0	0	0	0

Table 4.14

Table 4.15 summarizes these results:

Number of states	Reason for reduction	Resulting policy
101 x 23 = 2323	none: original problem	optimal
21 x 23 = 483	package weights were observed to be multiples of 5 tons	optimal
11 x 12 = 132	fine grid size	extremely near to optimal
5 x 5 = 25	coarse grid size	not remote from optimal

Table 4.15

It may be observed that a reduction of the problem to one-hundredth of its original size has brought about an approximate policy which is not remote from optimal.

Conclusion

The use of Lagrange multipliers and grid size reduction are only two of a number of methods of solving computational problems. Bellman and Dreyfus[7] consider various other methods and give a number of helpful flow charts related to specific problems. The best advice is to try to take account of the particular characteristics of each problem, since it is on them that the most appropriate computational method may depend.

5
Decision Analysis

Overview

This chapter is concerned with the relationship between dynamic programming and decision analysis, in which decisions are analyzed by portraying each possible sequence of decisions and their outcomes as a branch of a decision tree. The decision tree is a convenient way of representing and analyzing certain sequential decision problems: so, in many cases, is dynamic programming and one would expect the relationship to be close.

Example: marketing a new product

To illustrate the working of decision trees, we shall consider a simplified example. A foodstuffs manufacturer is contemplating the marketing of a new product. He knows (perhaps from past experience) that if he introduces the product, the probability that it will be successful (e.g. that it will increase gross profits by £30,000) is $\frac{1}{6}$. If it is unsuccessful (with probability $\frac{5}{6}$), then the manufacturer will lose his investment (let us say £10,000). Should he go ahead?

Suppose the manufacturer acts in accordance with the principle of maximizing his expected profit. His expected return from introduction is $\frac{1}{6} \times £30{,}000 + \frac{5}{6} \times -£10{,}000 = -£3{,}333$, which is less than zero, the profit resulting from staying as he is. Thus, other things being equal, he will not introduce the product as it will not be worth his while. We can put the situation in a table of returns (Table 5.1).

		State	
		1. successful ($p=\frac{1}{6}$)	2. unsuccessful ($p=\frac{5}{6}$)
Act	1. introduce product	+£30,000	−£10,000
	2. do not introduce	0	0

Table 5.1

If the manufacturer does not introduce the product he may of course be making a mistake, in that if he does introduce it, it might be a success and make him £30,000: all the manufacturer has done is act on the basis of expectations or play the odds. It would be worth something for him to know whether the product would be successful if he did introduce it. How much money should he be prepared to pay for this information? If in fact the product would be unsuccessful, then the money spent on information will be wasted for he does not intend to introduce the product anyway. However, if the product would be successful, then his decision will change: he will introduce it instead of not introducing it and make £30,000 minus whatever the information costs him. Since he believes that there is a 1 in 6 chance that the product will be successful, then there is a 1 in 6 chance that an infallible informer will tell him that it will be successful; therefore, so long as the information costs less than $\frac{1}{6}$ of £30,000 = £5,000 he should buy it and still expect (in the statistical sense) to make a profit.

We can show this in another way by extending the previous table to give Table 5.2, where £I is the cost of perfect information.

		State	
		1. successful ($p=\frac{1}{6}$)	2. unsuccessful ($p=\frac{5}{6}$)
Act	1. introduce product	£30,000	−£10,000
	2. do not introduce	0	0
	3. find out and then choose the better alternative	£(30,000 − I)	−£I

Table 5.2

It is worthwhile to choose act 3 so long as

$$\tfrac{1}{6}\,(30{,}000 - I) + \tfrac{5}{6}\,(-I) > 0$$

or

$$I < 5{,}000$$

In this case we say that £5,000 is the expected value of perfect information.

The information given in Tables 5.1 and 5.2 can also be presented in the form of a decision tree, in which acts and states are represented by branches; the tree for Table 5.1 looks like Figure 5.1.

The information in the tree is identical to that in the table: in the decision tree presentation the decision nodes are marked in the conventional way by squares and the event nodes by circles. To find the optimal act we work backwards from the extreme right branches (or twigs) to the trunk. Thus having computed $\frac{1}{6}$ x £30,000 + $\frac{5}{6}$ x −£10,000 and written the resulting expected return (−£3,333) at the appropriate event node, we compare it with the return from the alternative act (zero) and select that with the greater expected value (pruning the other branch). It is an easy exercise to draw a tree which includes branches relating to

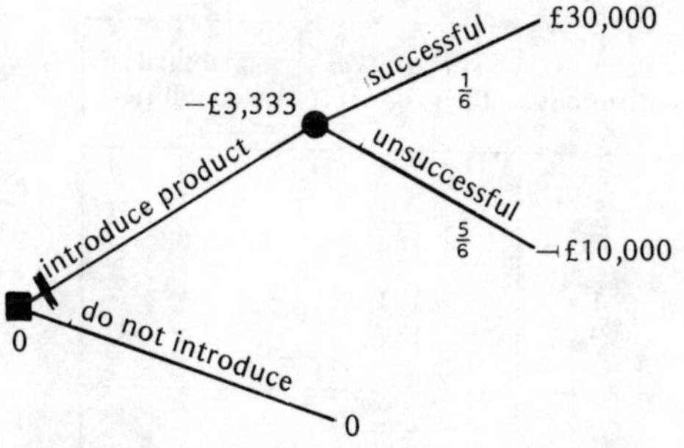

Figure 5.1

buying information and then choosing whether or not to introduce the product.

Clearly, perfect information is not usually to be had in life and we have to do the best we can with what we can get. The manufacturer, for example, might be able to draw on the opinion of a test panel. The panel might like the product, dislike it, or be indifferent to it: their attitude to the product will modify the manufacturer's estimate of the probability of its successful introduction. It may be that if the panel likes the product, then the manufacturer will consider the probability of success increased to fifty-fifty; if the panel dislikes it, then the manufacturer will consider the probability of success diminished to one in twelve; finally, if the panel is indifferent, then the manufacturer will change his estimate of success from one in six to one in three.

Suppose, finally, that the manufacturer thinks there is a one in ten chance that the panel will like the product and a one in six chance that they will be indifferent to it. Perhaps he assesses these probabilities in the light of his past experience with the panel's views on similar products. If this is so, then a decision tree can be drawn showing all the new possibilities open to the manufacturer.

It is worth noting that all the probability estimates given so far are not independent. In the (very) long run, out of 180 cases where this situation arises, there will be (on average)

18 cases where the panel likes the product
30 cases where the panel is indifferent
132 cases where the panel dislikes the product.

In the 18 cases where the panel likes the product, the product itself will be a success in 9 cases; in the 30 cases where the panel is indifferent, the product will be a success in 10 cases; in the 132 cases where the panel dislikes the product, the product will be a success in 11 cases. Thus in total, the product will be a success in 9 + 10 + 11 = 30 cases, a ratio of 30:180 or one in six, corresponding to the manufacturer's prior estimate. We may draw up Table 5.3 to illustrate the probabilities.

	Panel likes the product	Panel is indifferent	Panel dislikes the product	Marginal probabilities
Product is successful	$\frac{1}{20}$	$\frac{1}{18}$	$\frac{11}{180}$	$\frac{1}{6}$
Product is unsuccessful	$\frac{1}{20}$	$\frac{1}{9}$	$\frac{121}{180}$	$\frac{5}{6}$
Marginal probabilities	$\frac{1}{10}$	$\frac{1}{6}$	$\frac{11}{15}$	1

Table 5.3

The manufacturer's estimates of the conditional probabilities of success, dependent on the panel's opinion, enable us to split each of the marginal probabilities that the panel will like the product, not like it, or be indifferent, into two probabilities, thus for example:

probability that the panel likes the product and that the product is a success $= \frac{1}{2} \times \frac{1}{10} = \frac{1}{20}$

probability that the panel likes the product and that the product is not a success $= \frac{1}{2} \times \frac{1}{10} = \frac{1}{20}$

The total of the probabilities in the first row of the table is the marginal probability that the product is successful, or in figures

$$\frac{1}{20} + \frac{1}{18} + \frac{11}{180} = \frac{1}{6}$$

The marginal probability that the product is successful should be the same as the manufacturer's original estimate of the probability of having a successful product. If it is not, then the manufacturer's estimates are inconsistent and need to be adjusted until equality is achieved. The decision tree for the enlarged problem is shown in Figure 5.2.

The upper part of the tree is a copy of the earlier tree; the lower part is more complex because of the branches coming from the event node relating to the panel's opinion of the product. The computational procedure is exactly as before; for example, if the panel likes the product and the manufacturer introduces it, then the expected resulting profit is $\frac{1}{2} \times$ £30,000 + $\frac{1}{2} \times -$£10,000 = £10,000. £10,000 is more than zero, so the "do not introduce" branch is pruned. Two similar calculations enable us to compute the expected return from using the panel as $\frac{1}{10} \times$ £10,000 + $\frac{1}{6} \times$ £3,333 + $\frac{11}{15} \times$ £0 = £1,556; since £1,556 is more than zero, we prune the "do not use panel" branch. Some authors

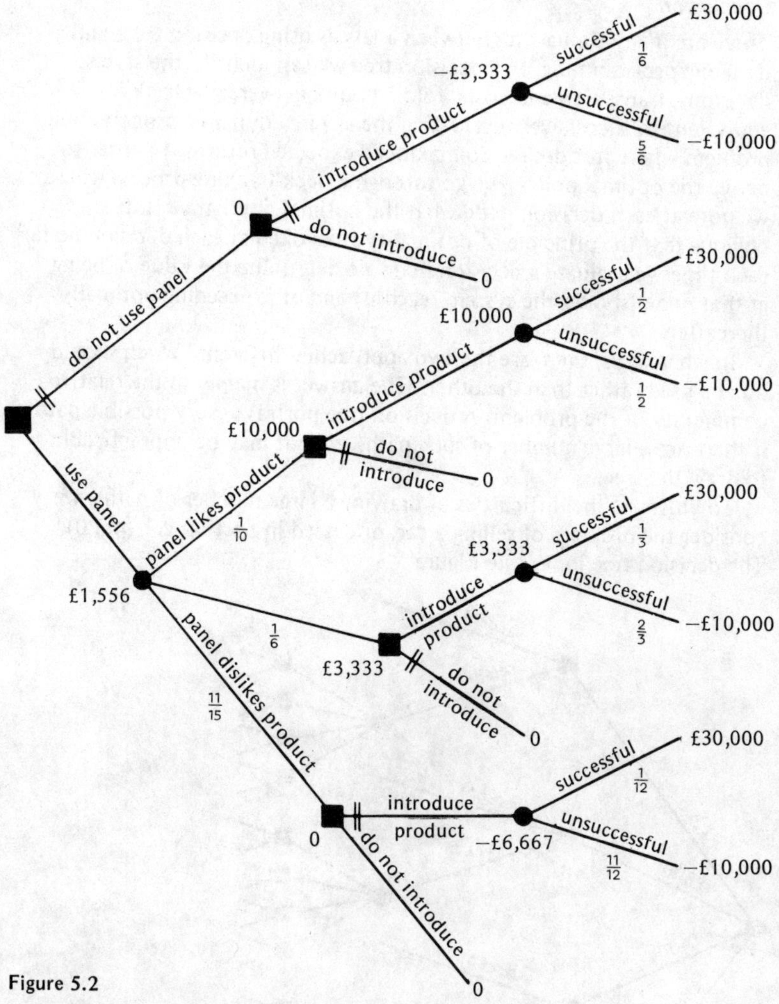

Figure 5.2

call this procedure averaging out and folding back.

Consequently the optimal policy is to use the panel and to introduce the product unless the panel dislikes it. The decision tree also tells us how much the panel's opinion is worth: on the basis of expected values, as long as the panel's opinion costs less than £1,556, then the manufacturer should seek it. It is worth noting, however, that the manufacturer may have other considerations to bear in mind such as alternative uses for his capital. As things are, his expected return on capital if he uses the panel is 15.56% and he may be able to do better than this elsewhere in his business. We have excluded such considerations from this example.

Conclusion

There are many similarities between analysis using decision trees and dynamic programming. In a decision tree we can identify the states, decisions, transitions and costs; folding out and averaging back is equivalent to successively evaluating the $f(.)$ in a dynamic programming problem where it is desired to maximize expected returns. In order to derive the optimal policy, we go through a back-tracking process where we note at each decision node what the optimal alternative is. It is obvious that the principle of optimality is invoked at each decision node: each time we evaluate a decision node we determine the value of being at that node (should the system reach it) and of proceeding optimally thereafter.

In what ways, then, are the two approaches different? When should one be used rather than the other? The answer is mainly in the relative complexity of the problem. A decision tree portrays every possible path; if there are a large number of such paths, then it may be impracticable to draw the tree.

To illustrate the difficulties of drawing a large number of paths, we consider the problem of selling a car, discussed in Section 2.1 (p. 20). The decision tree looks like Figure 5.3.

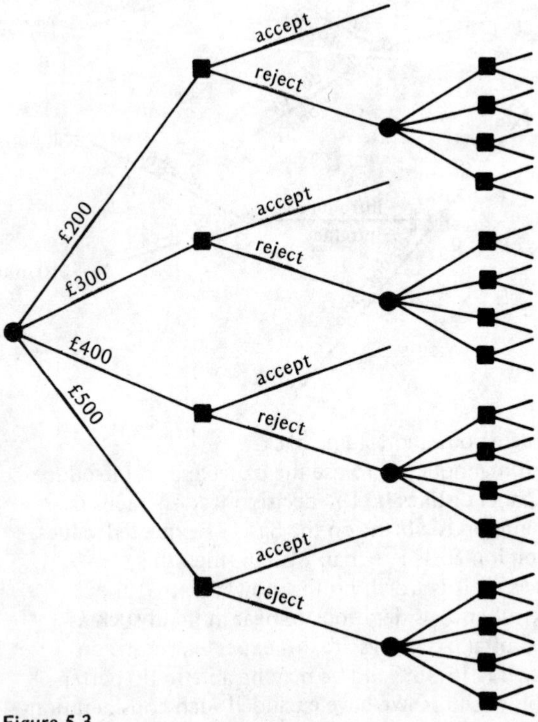

Figure 5.3

The tree is incomplete insofar as only two sets of decision nodes, corresponding to the first two days' bids, are shown. The repetitive nature of the diagram is apparent, however, and it is a feature of dynamic programming that it exploits this repetitiveness, through the principle of optimality, expressed in the functional equation.

On the other hand, a decision tree diagram can portray sequential problems in which the form of the state description differs at the various decision nodes. The foodstuffs manufacturer's problem is a case in point. The decision tree for this problem does not show the same repetitive pattern as the car selling problem and it is easy to think of ways in which information can be obtained about the probabilities of a successful or unsuccessful introduction which would make the tree still more irregular. For example, a second panel could be called on to give an opinion if and only if the original panel were indifferent. Such a problem might be difficult to solve using dynamic programming: nevertheless, the general computational principle is the same. Averaging out and folding back and then tracing the optimal policy is the same procedure as successively evaluating the state values and then backtracking.

Further Reading

The literature on dynamic programming and related topics is extensive and the following remarks represent a personal judgement.

The reader who wishes to extend his acquaintance with *applications* is recommended to read White[21] and Bellman and Dreyfus[7]. Chemical engineers will find Roberts[18] and (at an elementary level) Aris[3] well worthwhile. Bellman's books[4–6] contain many insights and some fascinating exercises, but for the non-mathematician they are hard going. Howard's book[10] is an object lesson in the readable presentation of difficult material and is highly recommended for anyone interested in the special topic of long-duration processes with stationary transition probabilities.

Bellman and Dreyfus[7] and Norman[14] deal with *computational methods in dynamic programming.* Pun[16] deals with dynamic programming as one of several competing optimization processes: this is a book for the applied mathematician.

Those interested in short expositions of *dynamic programming in relation to other methods of operational research* are well catered for. Ackoff and Sasieni[1], White Donaldson and Laurie[24], Makower and Williamson[12], and Mitchell[13] are all excellent texts.

Decision analysis is well treated by both Lindley[11] and Raiffa[17] in their short books. A more extensive treatment, with case studies, is given by Schlaifer[20]. White[22] and Fishburn[9] are two research monographs which deal, among other things, with the relationship of dynamic programming to decision theory.

The main *sources of up-to-date applications* are the abstracting services, of which the International Abstracts in Operational Research[8] and the Executive Sciences MS/OR Index[19] are the best known.

References

1 ACKOFF, R.I. and SASIENI, M.W. *Fundamentals of Operations Research,* Wiley, 1968.

2 AOKI, M. 'Dynamic Programming and Numerical Experimentation as Applied to Adaptive Control Systems', Ph. D. thesis, University of California, Los Angeles, 1960.

3 ARIS, R. *Discrete Dynamic Programming*, Blaisdell, 1964.

4 BELLMAN, R.E. 'Dynamic Programming and Adaptive Processes – Mathematical Foundations', *I.R.E. Trans. autom. Control, 5, 1, 1960.*

5 BELLMAN, R.E. *Dynamic Programming,* Princeton University Press, 1957.

6 BELLMAN, R.E. *Adaptive Control Processes – a Guided Tour,* Princeton University Press, 1961.

7 BELLMAN, R.E. and DREYFUS, S.E. *Applied Dynamic Programming,* Princeton University Press, 1962.

8 BRADLEY, H.E. (Ed.) *International Abstracts in Operations Research,* North-Holland.

9 FISHBURN, P.C. *Decision and Value Theory,* Wiley, 1964.

10 HOWARD, R.A. *Dynamic Programming and Markov Processes,* Technology Press and Wiley, 1960.

11 LINDLEY, D.V. *Making Decisions,* Wiley, 1971.

12 MAKOWER, M.S. and WILLIAMSON, E. *Operational Research,* English Universities Press, 1967.

13 MITCHELL, G.H. (Ed.) *Operational Research: Techniques and Examples,* English Universities Press, 1972.

14 NORMAN, J.M. *Heuristic Procedures in Dynamic Programming,* Manchester University Press, 1972.

15 POLYA, G. *How to Solve It,* Anchor, 1957.

16 PUN, L. *Introduction to Optimisation Practice,* Wiley, 1969.

17 RAIFFA, H. *Decision Analysis,* Addison-Wesley, 1968.

18 ROBERTS, S.M. *Dynamic Programming in Chemical Engineering and Process Control,* Academic Press, 1964.

19 ROSENTHAL, A.J. and D.S. (Eds.) *Operations Research/Management Science Yearbook,* Executive Science Inc., Whippany, N.J.

20 SCHLAIFER, R. *Analysis of Decisions Under Uncertainty,* McGraw-Hill, 1969.

21 WHITE, D.J. *Dynamic Programming,* Oliver and Boyd, 1969.
22 WHITE, D.J. *Decision Theory,* George Allen and Unwin, 1969.
23 WHITE, D.J. 'Studies in Dynamic Programming', Ph. D. thesis, University of Birmingham, 1961.
24 WHITE, D.J., DONALDSON, W.A. and LAURIE, N.L. *Operational Research Techniques,* Business Books, 1969.

Index

adaptive process 6,9
advertising budget 22
allocation 22
Aoki, M. 39
approximation in function space 48
approximation in policy space 48
averaging out and folding back 85

backtracking 15,22
backward contraction 40
backward recursion 45
barge 24,66,77
Bayes's theorem 31
Bellman, R.E. 1,6,9,39,80
brass strip 57

cannibals 63
car 3,18,86
computational effort 27,56,62, 65,72,77
computer 65
contractions (contracted policies) 3,40
critical value 19,37

decision 5
decision trees 81
deterministic process 6
dimensionality 32,65,77
directed states 52
discount factor 41
Dreyfus, S.E. 39,80

equipment replacement 3
explicit enumeration 62

final value systems 10,30
foodstuffs 81
formulation guidelines 28
FORTRAN 65
forward contraction 40
forward recursion 45

Googol 38
grid size 77

hillwalker 30
Howard, R.A. 51

ice-cream seller 4
imputed cost 72
inventory 66

knapsack 22

Lagrange multipliers 23,66
level 6
linear programming 22

marginal probability 84
marketing 81
missionaries 63
monotonicity 16

non-final value systems 10

orchestra 58
ordering of package types 27

policy 5
principle of optimality 1
puzzles 62

redundancy in computation 18
research and development budget 22
replacement 3
revised value 72
robustness 47
rolling mill 57
route 1,10,48,52

search 30
secretary 32
selling a car 3,18,86
sensitivity 45
sequential gaming 9
snooker balls 63
stage 4
state 4
stochastic process 6,8
submarine 30
substation 41

target state 33
test quantity 49,60
time horizon 45,51
transformations 6
troops 46
truncated policy 46

ullage 24

value iteration 48
value of information 82
vessels 63

White, D.J. 3,9,45,57